THE PENLAND
SCHOOL OF CRAFTS
Book of
JEWELRY MAKING

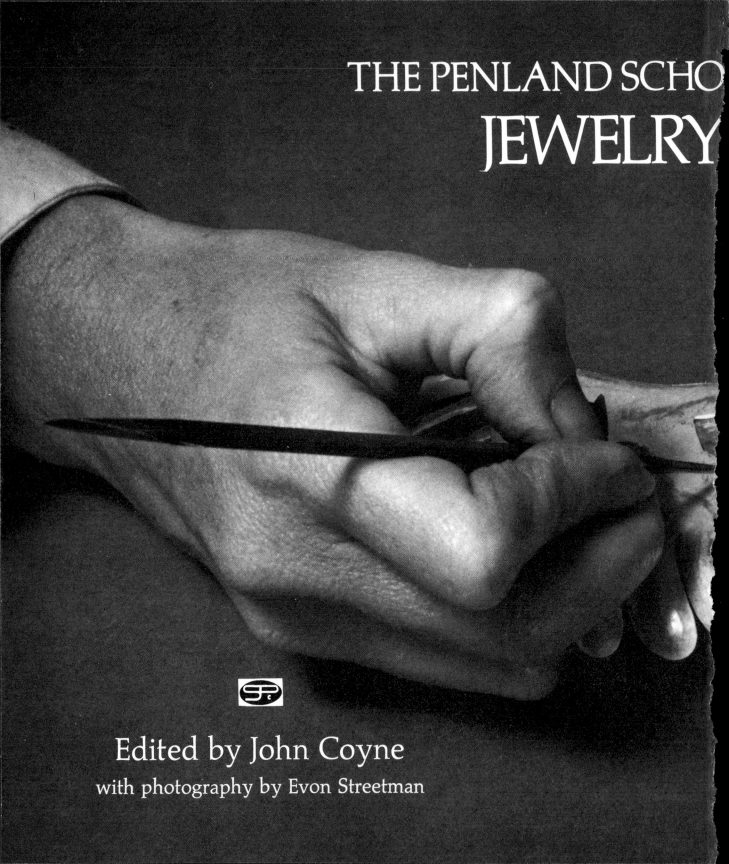

THE PENLAND SCHO
JEWELRY

Edited by John Coyne

with photography by Evon Streetman

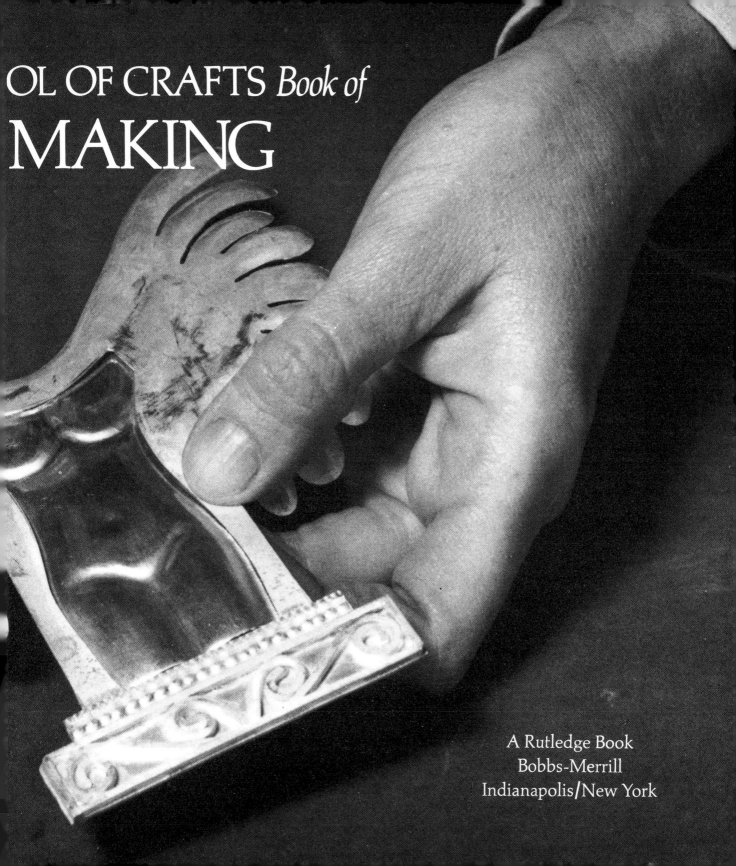

OL OF CRAFTS *Book of*
MAKING

A Rutledge Book
Bobbs-Merrill
Indianapolis/New York

Prepared and produced by Rutledge Books, 25 West
43 Street, New York, N.Y. 10036.

Published by The Bobbs-Merrill Company, Inc.,
Indianapolis/New York. ISBN: 0-672-51967-4.
Printed in Italy by Mondadori, Verona. First printing.

Library of Congress Cataloging in Publication Data
Coyne, John.
  The Penland School of Crafts book of jewelry making.

  A Rutledge book.
  1. Jewelry making.   I.   Penland School of Crafts,
Penland, N.C.   II.   Title.
TT212.C68   739.27   74-31333
ISBN 0-672-51967-4

This book is dedicated to the artist-craftsmen who have come to Penland to teach. They have freely shared their knowledge and talents so that others might learn a craft.

For their advice and assistance we would like to thank Jane Brown, Bonnie Ford, John Ehle, Peggy and Charlie Dysarts, Jessie McKinney, Betty Sue Hughes, Natalie Craig, Michael Robinson, Jane Hatcher, Jon Gray, Nancy Stanitz, Susan Silver, Frank Willis, Paul King, and Mary Cannon. Special thanks are due Claudia Kuehnl.

Contents

Editor's Note   9

Preface   11
William J. Brown

Materials   13

Sources of Supplies, Tools, and Equipment   15

Introduction   16
Mary Ann Scherr

Silver Triangular Bracelet   21
Mark Stanitz

Decorative Pocketknife   57
Gary Noffke

Penland Torso   77
Arline M. Fisch

Plexiglas Pin   113
Bob Ebendorf

Mirror Image 133
Eleanor Moty

Silver Forged Pin   153
Ronald Hayes Pearson

Helicoid Neckpiece   173
Heikki Seppä

Glossary of Jewelry-Making Terms   192

Editor's Note

Penland School has a very special place in the world of crafts. Year after year this school offers creative instruction in the major craft areas, taught by resident and visiting instructors who are among the finest in the world. Unfortunately, because of limited space, less than one thousand students each year are able to take advantage of Penland.

This space limitation was one reason why Bill Brown, Director of Penland, agreed to assist in the development of a series of books featuring the craftsmen of the school. He hopes that these books will be another way to share the talents of his unique faculty.

But Bill Brown and the craftsmen of Penland were not interested in doing just *how-to* books. They wanted a series that would accurately represent the school and also be a permanent example of the quality of instruction and the quality of creative work done here.

To achieve this, the instructors were asked to conceive of new pieces of jewelry, construct these pieces, and, by using photographs and text, clearly explain the technical processes involved. All this work was done at Penland. Evon Streetman, resident photographer, took the photographs that accompany the text.

We believe that the pieces created by these jewelers are exciting and challenging enough to intrigue both amateur and experienced jewelers into trying out the projects themselves. At the very least, we hope the reader will learn much about the techniques and possibilities of jewelry from this book.

Preface

Penland School of Crafts is a private, nonprofit organization in Penland, North Carolina, fifty-three miles northeast of Asheville and near the small town of Spruce Pine. It is the oldest, largest, and, we think, finest craft school in America.

Penland School was started by Miss Lucy Morgan in 1923. Miss Lucy once remarked to me that Penland was started "on a shoestring—and it frayed." Over the years it was built by Miss Lucy and others out of logs and bricks and glass and wallboard and pipe and nails and screws and other shoestrings, and keeping it all together has been a difficult task. But Penland was kept together, and it has grown. In 1923 Penland School was only one log building. Today we have thirty-three buildings on 380 acres of beautiful mountain land.

I have been at Penland School since 1962, and my wife and two boys and I have come to love it, and we have come to affectionately respect the people who travel to this high mountain community each year, where honest labor is particularly well favored. There is no finer community anywhere; there is no place where artistic, solid work is better appreciated, where artistic, solid people are more appreciated, or where I would rather work.

Thousands of people from North Carolina, from every state in the Union, and from over sixty foreign countries have come to this mountain community to learn to weave, to make pottery, and to work with wood, metal, glass, and stone. Some of these students have become professional craftsmen; many hundreds of others have developed an avocation that has been meaningful to them and their families.

We can now house, feed, and provide studio space for 130 people at each session. Last year we had over 700 students enrolled in our twelve courses. The only restriction we have is that a student must be at least eighteen years of age. We have college and art school students, grandmothers, doctors, lawyers, teachers (and they come in all colors)—anyone who wants to learn.

Students work an average of sixty hours per week in ceramics, weaving, glassblowing, graphics, photography, woodworking, vegetable dyeing, lapidary, plastics, jewelry, enameling, and sculpture. We have six sessions of two and three weeks during the summer and two special eight-week concentration courses in the spring and fall. For those who wish, both graduate and undergraduate college credit may be received for their work.

Throughout the year Penland sponsors a unique craftsmen's fellowship program for a limited number of well-trained craftsmen. These young people design, produce, and learn to market their work, using our facilities, for which they pay a nominal fee. Thus far we have helped ten craftsmen; they now own and operate their own studios and make a living producing their own work.

Penland has the finest faculty of any institution of its kind in the world. No other school could afford the salaries of the over seventy faculty members we have here during our sessions. We can't afford them either, so we don't pay them! They work for room and board, plus travel expenses. They do this because they believe that what we are doing here is worthwhile. These noted people donate the greatest gift we receive: their time, talent, and knowledge. They are the major reason for our success.

It is not our plan to increase the size of Penland, for it is felt that larger size would spoil the flavor of the school and destroy its educational quality. We must continue to grow in quality and to contribute in special ways to creativity in the crafts.

One way we hope to contribute is through a series of craft books. This particular book on jewelry is one of the first in this series. Of the many fine jewelers who teach at Penland we have asked these artists to share their knowledge through instructional material and photographs.

As an educational institution, we think it is one of our responsibilities to make available the unique talents we have at Penland. If it is not possible for everyone to come and study here at our mountain school, we hope then that they can share, through these books, in the lives and skills of these talented people who have made Penland School of Crafts such an extraordinary place.

WILLIAM J. BROWN
Director

Materials

Supplies

The following items are used by Penland craftsmen to produce the pieces of jewelry described in this book. They need not all be purchased at once, but may be obtained as needed for the home workshop.

Binding wire: Used to hold metals in position during soldering; also used for stringing objects that are to be dipped in plating solutions and cleaners. Supplied in ½-pound spools; 18 to 22 gauges most useful.

Borax: Used as a flux by mixing with water to form a paste. Powdered household borax can be used.

Emery: Available as a powder, or glued to paper or cloth. Emery paper and cloth are graded by numbers, from 4/0 (finest) to 3 (coarsest). For general use, Nos. ½ to 2 are recommended. An emery stick is formed by wrapping the paper around a piece of wood.

Epoxy: Used as a glue. Available in tubes in various setting times: 5-minute, 10-minute, and 1-hour. Can be purchased at any hardware store.

Handy Flux: A commercially prepared flux, available in both paste and liquid forms; a 1-pound can is recommended. Flux acts as a heat indicator and prevents oxidation of the metal during soldering.

Liver of sulfur: A chemical, potassium sulfide, used to give silver and copper a bluish black finish. Prepared by dropping a ½-inch cube of the chemical into a quart of hot water, then adding the object, which is removed when it turns bluish black. Larger objects, which cannot be placed in the solution, can be finished by dipping steel wool into the chemical and then rubbing the solution on the object. Available in 4-ounce and 1-pound jars.

Pitch: Used as a base or support material for chasing and repoussé work. Homemade pitch can be mixed from 2 pounds pitch, 3 pounds plaster of paris, and 2 ounces tallow. Burgundy pitch is a preferred commercial product; it can be obtained from supply houses, usually in 1¾-pound containers. Three containers are recommended.

Polishing compounds: Pumice: a fast-cutting abrasive used to prepare silver objects for tripoli and rouge. Can be purchased in lump form, in cake form, or as a powder. Powdered pumice is available in various grades, from extra coarse (2) to extra fine (2F). In lump form it is used for filling an annealing pan.

Rouge: a synthetic iron oxide mixed with grease to form bars for easy handling. Red rouge is recommended. A ¼-pound bar is sufficient.

Tripoli: a silicon substance that removes emery marks and fine scratches. It is mixed with grease to form bars or cakes for easy handling. A ¼-pound bar is sufficient.

Solder: There are two divisions of solder—hard and soft. Hard solders—alloys of silver, copper, and zinc—are high melting, are used on silver, copper, brass, bronze, and nickel silver when very strong joints are required. Comes in four grades—extra-easy, easy, medium, and hard; in three forms—wire, strip, and sheet, the second two being the most popular; and in various gauges, the most common being 20 to 28. Strip solder is sold in multiples of 1-foot lengths. Solder is also sold by weight; 1 ounce of each grade is recommended.

Soft solders are alloys of tin and lead and have a low melting point. Can be purchased in various forms: wire, bar, hollow wire containing flux, and small pieces. Soft solders are rarely used, except for soldering operations performed after enameling.

Sparex: A granular dry acid compound—a safe substitute for sulfuric acid—specially made for pickling, cleaning, and removing surface oxidation and scale from copper and silver. Noninflammable, nonexplosive. A 2½-pound can makes 1 gallon of solution, sufficient for the beginning craftsman.

Steel wool: Available in coarse, medium, fine, and extra-fine grades. May be purchased at any hardware store.

Tools and Equipment

Annealing pan: Used for annealing metals—softening by heating—as well as in soldering. The pan is filled with lump pumice and rotates on its base.

Bench anvil: A small jeweler's anvil used for shaping, stretching, and forging metal sheet and wire.

Bench block: Any hardened steel block, 2½ by 2½ inches square and at least 1 inch thick. Used for flattening, forging, and stamping metal.

Bench vise: Most useful is a jawed bench vise at least 3 inches wide.

Buffing wheels: The best sizes are 3, 4, and 5 inches. The wheels are available in stitched muslin, unstitched muslin, slotter, rockhard felt, bristle, felt ring buff, and felt stick. Most jewelers use unstitched wheels, with rouge as a polishing compound. Bristle brushes are used to get into crevices, felt and wood wheels for sharp corners. The insides of rings are polished with tapered felt or wood mandrels or with bristle brushes.

Chasing hammer: Has a wide, flat face and a long, thin-necked handle. A 1-inch face is the most useful.

Chasing tools: Can be purchased from jewelry supply houses, but many jewelers prefer to make their own. A basic list of chasing tools contains between fifteen and twenty instruments. The fundamental shapes are: liner, planisher, matting, doming, and dapping.

Combination bench pin and anvil: Useful for filing, sawing, and hammering.

Dapping block and punches: Dapping blocks, used to form semi-spheres, are made of steel, lead, or wood. The punches come in sets of twelve, eighteen, twenty-four, and thirty.

Files: There are two classifications of files—Swiss and American. The coarseness of a Swiss file is marked by a number system, with No. 00 the coarsest and No. 6 the smoothest. The coarseness of American files is specified by name: rough, bastard, second cut, smooth, and super-smooth.

Files have different kinds of cuts, among them, single, double, vixen, and rasp. A single-cut file has a single row of parallel teeth running the entire cutting length. A double-cut file has an additional row of teeth cut at a 60-degree angle to the first row; Swiss files are all double cut. A vixen-cut file has a single row of curved teeth running across its entire length. Rasp-cut files have short, raised teeth.

Files come in a variety of cross-sectional shapes. The most common are: round, barrette, half-round, square, crossing, three-corner, knife, equaling, and crochet.

A needle file is used for finishing small and delicate objects. A common size is 16 centimeters, with a cutting length of $2\frac{3}{4}$ inches.

A beginning jeweler should have a small assortment of files, depending on need. Most recommended are a No. 2 and a No. 3 Swiss-cut, 6-inch half-round file. Handles may be purchased at any hardware store.

Flexible shaft: Used for polishing, drilling, and stone setting.

Jeweler's saws and blades: Saw frames are made in a range of depths, from $2\frac{1}{4}$ to 6 inches. Most recommended are a $2\frac{1}{4}$-inch frame for close jewelry work and a 4-inch frame for larger pieces.

Jeweler's saw blades vary in size from No. 8/0, the thinnest, to No. 14, the thickest. For very fine pierced work, a No. 8/0 is used. General work in silver and gold requires blades from 3/0 to 2. Saw blades should be purchased in quantity, as they are easily broken.

Pickle pan: Pickling is the process of removing flux and oxide from metal by means of acid. A pickle solution of water and sulfuric acid, or the commercially prepared Sparex No. 2, is boiled in a lead, Pyrex, or ceramic crucible. A covered Pyrex dish is used most commonly.

Pitch bowl: The ideal form for holding pitch is the chaser's pitch bowl, made of cast iron in diameters of 6 and 8 inches and set on a cord or leather ring base.

Plate shear: Used for cutting sheets of metal; particularly useful for cutting sheet solder.

Pliers: There are two types of pliers, one with parallel jaw action and one with jaws that pivot around a rivet. Standard common pliers come in lengths from 3 to 6 inches; 5-inch pliers are most commonly used by jewelers. Pliers can be round, chain, flat, snipe, or half-round. A beginning jeweler should have chain and round-nose pliers.

Polishing machine: Almost any electric split-phase motor can be made into a buffing machine by attaching a tapered spindle, which holds the buffing wheels. A double-shafted $\frac{1}{3}$ hp motor is preferred by many craftsmen. A variable speed motor with speeds up to 3600 rpm is desirable.

Raising mallets: A rawhide mallet is used where work must not be marked or injured. A forming mallet is made of wood and is used on sheet metal.

Ring mandrel: Made of hardened tool steel and used for shaping, straightening, and enlarging rings; also used for making bezels. Mandrels come in graduated plain and graduated grooved shapes.

Rolling mill: Geared hand mills are available for shops. The best is a flat-and-square mill combination—the flat for reducing the thickness of sheet metal, the square for forming square bars. Rolling mills can be fitted with interchangeable rolling bars. Some are made just for wire, some for a combination of sheet and wire.

Setting tools: Used for setting stones. Can be ground to shape from square and round engraving tools; usually made of steel. The burnisher, the most common, is an oval-shaped polished and hardened piece of tool steel with either a straight or a curved tip.

Soldering equipment: The least expensive is a mouth blowpipe, in which gas is connected to the side of the pipe and air is blown in by mouth from the end to produce flame. The gas can be obtained from the kitchen gas range by disconnecting one of the burners. If gas is not available, a Prest-o-lite outfit with a pressure regulator is suggested; it is easy to operate and comparatively inexpensive to use. The Prest-o-lite tank contains acetylene gas dissolved in carbon tetrachloride and is available in several sizes: a "B" tank with a No. 2 torch tip for detailed work and a No. 5 or No. 6 tip for large work.

Stakes: The three common kinds are: a T-type raising stake, 12 inches long, for forming and planishing conical work, heavy rings, and bases of bowls; a planishing stake, 2 to $2\frac{1}{2}$ inches in diameter, round or domed, used for shaping; and a beakhorn stake with a square taper, from $\frac{1}{2}$ to 1 inch diameter.

Tweezers: The home workshop requires at least two cross-lock tweezers, one copper pickle tongs, and a $4\frac{3}{4}$ - or 5-inch straight tweezers.

Workbench: Any bench can be used; the best has a hardwood top and a sliding tray of galvanized iron to catch filings for gold and platinum work.

Sources of Supplies, Tools, and Equipment

Materials may be ordered through the mail from catalogs issued by these houses.

Screen Process Supplies
  Manufacturing Company
1199 East 12th Street
Oakland, California 94606

D. V. Pederson
1420 University Avenue
San Diego, California 92103

Swartchild and Company
22 West Madison Street
Chicago, Illinois 60602

C. R. Hill Company
2734 West 11 Mile Road
Berkley, Michigan 48072

Brookstone Company
16 Brookstone Building
Peterborough, New Hampshire 03458

William Dixon, Inc.
750 Washington Avenue
Carlstadt, New Jersey 07072

Anchor Tool and Supply Company
Box 265
Chatham, New Jersey 07928

The Craftool Company
1 Industrial Avenue
Woodridge, New Jersey 07075

United States General Supply
  Corporation
100 General Place
Jericho, New York 11753

All-Craft Tool and Supply Company
15 West 45 Street
New York, New York 10036

Gamzon Brothers
21 West 46 Street
New York, New York 10036

Paul H. Gesswein and Company
235 Park Avenue South
New York, New York 10003

I. Shor
71 Fifth Avenue
New York, New York 10003

Kraft Korner
5860 Mayfield Road
Cleveland, Ohio 44124

Ohio Jeweler's Supply
1000 Schofield Building
Cleveland, Ohio 44115

Keystone Jeweler's Supply Company
715 Sansom Street
Philadelphia, Pennsylvania 19106

Silvo Hardware
107-109 Walnut Street
Philadelphia, Pennsylvania 19106

Swest, Inc.
1080 Composite Drive
Dallas, Texas 75220

Sax Arts and Crafts
P. O. Box 2002
Milwaukee, Wisconsin 53201

Gold & Silver

Goldsmith Brothers
111 North Wabash Avenue
Chicago, Illinois 60602

Handy & Harman
830 Third Avenue
New York, New York 10022

Southwest Refining Company
P. O. Box 2010
Dallas, Texas 75221

Copper & Brass

William Dixon, Inc.
750 Washington Avenue
Carlstadt, New Jersey 07072

Introduction
Mary Ann Scherr

Mary Ann Scherr is an internationally known artist-designer who teaches at Kent State University. In the last few years she has been experimenting with making jewelry not only for adornment, but as vessels to hold new instruments to monitor the heart and regulate the heartbeat and as indicators of air pollution. Mary Ann Scherr has taught at Penland School of Crafts for eleven years. She is a member of the Society of North American Goldsmiths.

No one can really say how jewelry began, but from earliest times, jewelry served very special purposes for its wearers. It could be a status symbol—the warrior with a collar of ninety lion's teeth was more respected in his tribe than the man with a collar of only fifty—or it could be a magical protector—such as the totem figure worn into battle. During the Middle Ages, for example, jewelry served both as physical protection and as indicator of status in battle, for the metal armor worn by warriors (and often their horses as well) was highly decorated by techniques still used in jewelry making today.

From an early time, too, jewelry was used to symbolize private relationships, in the form of tokens such as rings, which became visible and public proclamations of such relationships.

Basically, the function of jewelry has changed very little over the centuries. Today, as in the past, the jewelry a person wears makes a public statement about him. It may signify his wealth, identify a tribal connection, a religious belief, or a social attitude, or proclaim his marital status. Most importantly, jewelry shows how the wearer feels about himself and how he expects others to feel about him.

A modern jeweler is quickly linked to the history and philosophy of craft. The tools, techniques, and materials he uses are part of this heritage, for they have not changed much over the centuries. The advent of electric power has led to greater flexibility with some techniques, and ancient methods have been varied to produce new forms. But basically, tools and methods have merely been refined; few really new ones have been invented. Our most common jewelers' metals still rank as they did in pre-Columbian and biblical times.

However, the limited availability and rising costs of favored metals today are likely to produce changes. As gold and silver grow scarcer, we will find ourselves discovering and confronting challenges in new alloys and other materials. Since each metal imposes its own qualities

17

on the craftsman, these inherent qualities will direct what can be produced. Man-made products, too—of current and future technology—will enforce their qualities on the jeweler and direct his course of work.

Though new materials may appear on the scene, our materials and methods today are still basically those of the past—so what about jewelry has really changed since Cleopatra's time? It is probably the attitude of the jeweler himself. Unlike the craftsman of the past, whose pieces were often "commemorative" works designed for a specific occasion or display, today's jeweler has both the freedom and the desire to make jewelry as a personal expression.

I and other metalsmiths in this book share much together. We are all responsive to and, indeed, dependent on the legacy of jewelers of centuries ago, but we are people of the twentieth century, dealing with ideas that take jewelry and metalworking beyond fashion and into the realm of personal expression and invention. We also share a common tendency, it seems to me, to be rather private people. Perhaps that is because of the intimacy of our relationship to the materials we use and the fact that we deal primarily with detail in a confined context.

But what we have shared most joyfully—each of us individually—is the experience of working and teaching at Penland. We are not all there at the same time, of course, but what happens for each of us seems to have a common feeling, so that I think I can speak for the other instructors whose work you will get to know in this book.

The Penland experience permits us to maintain our basic privacy while becoming part of an atmosphere that is almost explosive with ideas. At Penland, labels and time almost cease to exist. We learn along with the people we teach. It's an environment where learning occurs without formal academic limitations and where teaching loses its formality, in a momentum generated by the thrust of idea and counteridea.

Perhaps the magnetism and vitality of Penland come from the astonishing variety of methods and techniques one meets there. Part of it certainly comes from the respect of one craftsman for another: the ceramist's 3 A.M. conversation may stimulate the weaving student who, at breakfast, may inspire a photographer who, by noon, may have attempted a new printing experiment and discussed it with the glassblower, and so on. I may not return from Penland doing anything the glassblower does, but his attitude about his work affects me, just as mine affects him, because we are bouncing ideas off each other in our mutual search for new ideas.

And each Penland instructor approaches his own craft in an

individual way. The jewelers in this book work with a variety of materials, each in a differing direction, to expand the possibilities in the spectrum of goldsmithing, silversmithing, whitesmithing, and blacksmithing.

My own work, most recently, has taken me into jewelry forms that not only adorn the wearer, but respond to the wearer's external and even internal atmosphere. Creating jewelry that actually displays the wearer's heartbeat, for instance, has given me an opportunity to work with technicians in fields far different from my own: electromechanical engineers, biologists, physicists, and medical doctors. Thus the work has provided still another form of personal expansion for me.

I don't believe any artist can stand still, no matter what his craft. That is one reason why the Penland experience propels us to be open to the expanding capacity of the tools, methods, and materials we work with as well as to people who can offer new ideas. Because I have challenged myself over the years by experimenting with new materials, I've never had a chance to feel static. And I think the same rhythm of change and experiment is found in the other jewelers in this book.

Actually, I find it difficult to talk about myself and my craft. It's hard for me to make what I do seem important, because what I do comes naturally. I hope I never outgrow the need to change, so that each piece I produce will be significant in itself—both to its eventual owner and to me as its designer.

When I try to find a pigeonhole for myself in the current art world, that, too, is difficult. I am artisan, artist, and technician, with very specific professional standards. But I think of myself as a designer first, because I feel that when design and technique compete with one another, design is the only thing that matters, and perhaps the only way the artist marks a work as truly his own.

And perhaps that is the only message I can offer the would-be jeweler or craftsman. This book is full of techniques, none of which is particularly difficult to learn. But techniques, no matter how well mastered, are valueless without the personal design and inspiration of the individual craftsman.

Tools, materials, and methods have their limitations, but the craftsman who remains open to new ideas, who respects the rich history of his craft and investigates its implications while responding to suggestions from the present, who experiments to broaden his sensitivity to design, can develop unlimited capacity to create in almost any field.

Perhaps it takes a place like Penland to make the truth of such a statement come to life.

Silver Triangular Bracelet
Mark Stanitz

Mark Stanitz is a young craftsman who is currently the jeweler in residence at Penland School of Crafts. He has been working on an experimental basis with a new form of plating, which achieves, in a quick and efficient way, the look of the ancient Japanese wood-grain style.

Mark Stanitz was born in Cleveland, Ohio. He received both his B.F.A. and his Master's degrees from Kent State University, Kent, Ohio.
His work has been exhibited at the Piedmont Craft Guild in Winston-Salem, North Carolina, 1974; the Cleveland May Show in Cleveland, Ohio, 1974; and the Catholic University Show in Washington, D.C., 1974.
His work is in the collections of Mr. and Mrs. Sheldon Franz; Mr. and Mrs. Ronald Propst; and Mr. and Mrs. Andrew Novick.
Mark Stanitz has taught at Kent State University and Penland School of Crafts, where he is now resident jeweler. He lives in Penland, North Carolina.

Silver Triangular Bracelet. Sterling silver, electroplated silver and copper beads, opals

I start my pieces by establishing a basic concept of what they will be. Very rarely do I have all aspects of the design decided on before I begin. I also do not pick up a pencil until I have the essence of the piece firmly in mind; I believe that as soon as I pick up a pencil and begin to draw, I limit the possibilities of the piece. Also, by picturing the piece in my mind it is quicker for me to conceptualize the total design.

While I'm conceptualizing I am thinking also of the materials I will use and the technical problems that might occur, for the piece has to be technically possible as well as esthetically pleasing before I can start. When that combination is reached, I begin and, when necessary for layout purposes, commit the design to paper.

Very rarely do I have a definite concept of the end result when I start, since I often change my mind while working, sometimes because of the requirements of the material. If I have the feeling of the basic object firmly in my mind and can see it, that's all I need. And that's the best way to begin.

With this particular piece I have a pattern that must be sawed out of metal. The piece is a bracelet that is going to be made out of two triangular, contoured shapes. Therefore, I know I need two identical pieces of metal. I take the drawing I've made and apply Sanding Disc Cement to it and place it on the metal. (Contact paper works just as well for this process.) The metal I've selected is 18-gauge sterling silver, which is strong enough for the bracelet I'm creating.

When cutting the metal I start slightly outside the line I want. (Figure 1) This allows me later to use a file, which naturally is a slower cutting action but more precise.

For this cutting I use a jeweler's saw. There are three throat sizes available: four, six, or eight inches deep, which are adequate for most cuts. The best structural strength sterling to use is 18-gauge—it's strong enough to make just about any form. Twenty-gauge is usually too light to handle tension, and 16-gauge, though very strong, adds too much weight to the object. Eighteen-gauge is .040 thick, or 4/100 inch. For this particular piece and the cutting required, I am using a 2/0 size blade in a four-inch-deep throat saw. Saw blades range from 4 to 4/0, 4 being the heaviest.

A lot of people wax their saw blades for cutting. I don't. I get a much quicker cutting action by not lubricating the blade at all. If you do use wax, beeswax is very good. You can't cut as quickly, but it lessens the chance of breaking the saw blades. (Saw blades are easily broken,

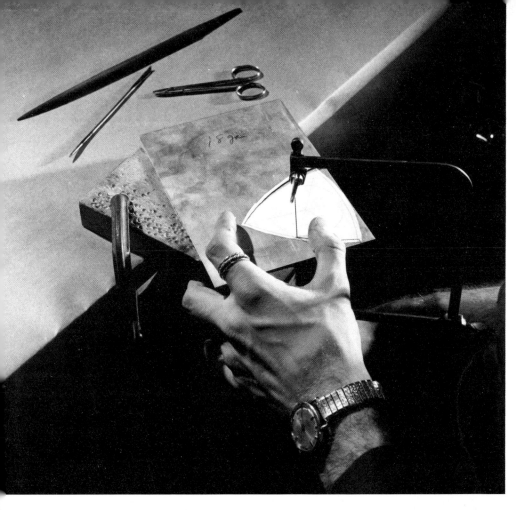

Figure 1. The silver is cut from a pattern, with the cuts made slightly outside the line.

Figure 2a. The second piece is traced from the first one to ensure that the two are identical.

especially when you are an inexperienced, beginning jewelry maker.)

When the saw reaches the corner, a different method of cutting is required. In this case the turn is sharper than a 90-degree angle. I hold the saw at the corner and make short, quick strokes, while slowly rotating the saw. This creates a small hole right where the blade is sitting—then it's possible to turn the saw and continue the cut.

After the first blank is cut, I lay it on the base metal and trace the second piece. (Figure 2) I use a dental pick to draw on the metal. I don't want the pick to be too sharp because a point tends to jab into the metal. I get a sharp point, then make it slightly round by working it over on a hard felt wheel. I try to get the point round, like a ballpoint pen, but smaller. This allows the drawing on the metal to be very smooth and easy. In drawing I move the scribe toward myself as much as possible so that I am drawing in the opposite direction from the way the scribe is pointing. When I have the two rough shapes cut out, I glue them together

Figure 2b. The second piece is cut from the traced pattern.

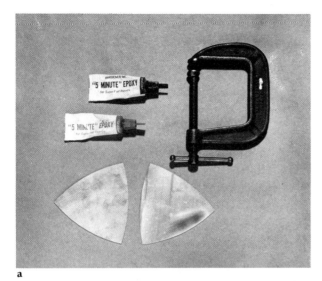

a

b

Figure 3. The pieces are cemented together and then held tight with clamps while the cement hardens.

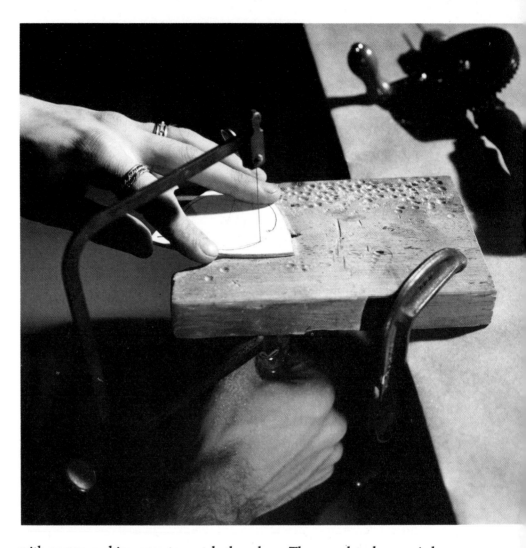

Figure 4. The center circle is cut, leaving room for filing.

with epoxy, making sure to match the edges. They need to be epoxied so that the outside edges can be filed, and the inside hole cut, to an identical shape. It's important for the two holes to be centered exactly, because a cylinder has to be sunk down through the middle. By epoxying the metal together, identical holes can be sawed.

The best epoxy to use is 5-Minute Epoxy. It sets up quickly, and it creates a bond strong enough to hold the metal during sawing. The epoxy is mixed with a match or small stick—something disposable. The setting time can be speeded up by heating the epoxy: just lower a light bulb close to the metal or place the metal near a heating duct. Regular epoxy can be speeded up this way if 5-Minute Epoxy isn't available.

I am not concerned with covering the whole piece with epoxy. I just want to be sure that the edges of both pieces meet correctly, because I have only 1/64 inch to play with (Figure 3)—the distance outside the line that defines the final shape. By matching perfectly I cut down on the filing. After epoxying, the piece is set in clamps and given time to harden.

In cutting out the center hole of the bracelet the first step is to drill a small hole so that I can get the saw blade into the interior of the metal. I create a slight hole with a center punch. This allows the drill to be started without sliding around the metal. I cut the hole with a high-

Figure 5. The file is held level when strokes are made.

Figure 6. The inside circle must be at a 90-degree angle to the surface of the blanks.

Figure 7. The piece is
fluxed before heating.

Figure 8. The epoxy is burned off by heating the piece to 350 degrees.

speed twist drill. The drill bit is designed to cut metal and is 1/16 inch in diameter, large enough to get the saw blade through. I next take the bottom end of the blade out of the frame, slip it through the hole, and reattach the blade. I cut the circle out (Figure 4), but stay shy of the line actually wanted. Once again, I will file this true.

The file will cut only on a forward stroke. The file I use first is a medium-toothed file, eight inches long. It has one flat side and one that's half round. I use this type because I have outside edges that are convex, and on a convex surface I use the flat side of the file. On the inside, which is concave, I use the convex side of the file. Periodically I'll pick up

Figure 9. The metal is shaped with a rawhide mallet.

Figure 10. The tips are ground flat to establish a wider edge.

the piece and check the edges. When there are even file marks on both edges of the two pieces, I consider the piece finished.

I put the piece in the vise to knock down the excess metal quickly (Figure 5) and then shift to a finer file. As I make a stroke I always move the file from side to side so that I don't create grooves at any one point. The inside of the circle is faster to finish because the pieces were cut out together.

The inside edge of the circle should be at a 90-degree angle to the surface of the blanks. (Figure 6) This is necessary because a cylinder, which will form the sleeve, has to sit inside. I give the file less pressure

Figure 11. Wire solder is used on easily reached joints.

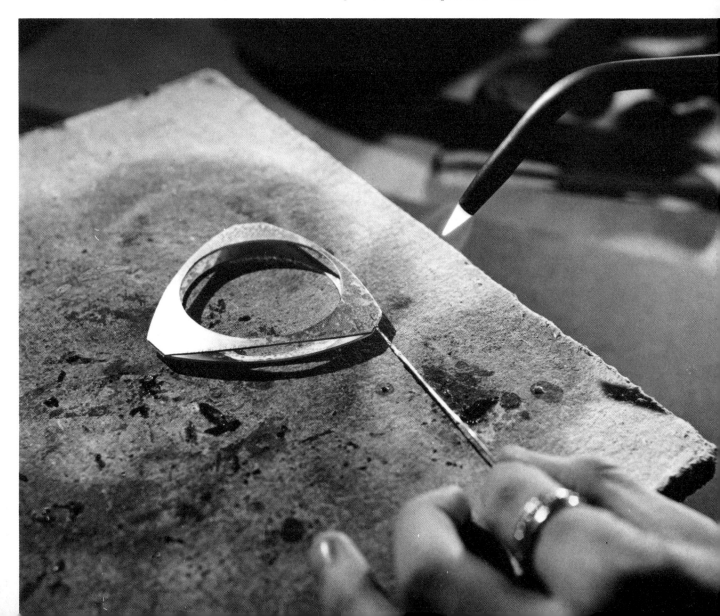

on the inside, covering only one inch at a swing. This is done because the convex side of the file has only a small point in contact with the metal and I do not want it to make any grooves.

Before splitting the pieces by heating them with a torch, I have to flux the metal. (Figure 7) Sterling silver is an alloy that contains copper, and when copper is taken up to a high temperature it oxidizes and forms heat scale. This leaves a dark gray, shadowy effect on the surface of the silver, which is very difficult to get out of a finished product, especially if it has a high polish. By fluxing the metal, and thereby not allowing air to reach it when it's heated, copper oxidation can't occur.

Handy paste flux, which is what I'm using, is made primarily out of borax. I use it here for two reasons: to protect the metal from oxidizing, and to act as a heat indicator. When the flux is heated to 1100 degrees, it turns glassy and flows out clear like water. At 1200 degrees, the sterling silver anneals. So by watching the condition of the flux you can judge the condition of the silver.

It is best to work on an asbestos board, as asbestos is a very good insulator; it doesn't conduct heat well. If you heat a piece of metal on it, it won't pull the heat off. To heat the piece I use an acetylene and air torch, with a large No. 4 tip, because I want to heat it quickly.

The splitting takes place at about 350 degrees, when the epoxy is burned off. (Figure 8) After the pieces are split they are dropped into a pickle solution heated to about 160 degrees. The solution is made of water and Sparex No. 2, which is a commercially available synthetic acid compound that does not attack the metal but does remove surface oxidation from any nonferrous metal (silver, copper, brass, bronze, gold). Pickle solutions should be used in copper, porcelain, Pyrex, or stainless steel containers, and when mixing, the acid should always be added to the water, not the water to the acid.

The piece is left in the pickle for about five minutes, rinsed, then dried. The only other type of metal—other than the piece itself—that should be put in the pickle is copper. If steel tongs are used to retrieve the metal, a thin flash of copper appears on the metal being pickled. (If the copper flash is left on, a weak solder joint could result.)

Next, the two pieces are contoured over a rounded stake. (Figure 9) A rawhide mallet is used for this job because it is softer than silver and will not mar the metal. The contour shape is achieved by striking the metal with glancing blows. Since the metal has already been annealed by the heating, it is easy to work with.

The two contoured pieces are then placed on emery paper and the

Figure 12. The cylinder is cut from sterling silver sheet.

Figure 13. The cylinder is soldered with medium wire solder.

Figure 14. The cylinder is pounded into shape with a rawhide mallet over a mandrel.

Figure 15. Square wire is soldered to the bracelet to give it depth.

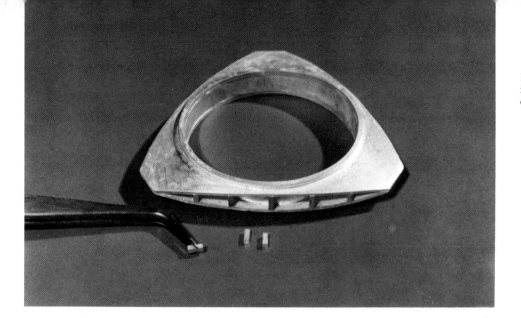

Figure 16. Pressure fit is required for the placement of the posts.

Figure 17. One side at a time is soldered.

tips are ground down so that they are flat and have a wider edge for more solder contact. (Figure 10)

Before soldering, the surface of the pieces must be cleaned with steel wool so that flux will adhere to it. Flux is used in soldering for three purposes: as a heat indicator, as a solder flow inducer, and as an anti-heat scale agent. The entire surface must be kept covered with flux so that air can't get to the hot silver.

I use medium solder for this job, as it melts at around 1335 degrees. I use it in the form of wire instead of chips, because the joints are on the outside and easy to reach. (Figure 11) Once the metal is heated I apply the solder. With the proper use of the torch, the solder can be pulled directly through the joints, since solder always flows toward the source of heat. Silver solder will form a bond with metal-to-metal contact that is about 44,000 pounds per square inch.

As the piece is heated evenly, the first change that occurs is that the water is driven from the flux, leaving a frosty white powder on the metal. This occurs at 212 degrees. The next change is at 1100 degrees: the flux turns to a perfectly clear liquid and flows over the surface. When the metal reaches 1335 degrees I apply the solder. The metal at this point has changed to a dull carrot glow. Being careful to keep the metal from getting too hot, I apply the solder quickly and back off, then immediately put the hot metal into the pickle and let it set for a few minutes.

The next part of the bracelet to be made is the cylinder. I cut this part from 18-gauge silver sheet to a depth of 23/64 inch and a length of 7.1 inches. (Figure 12) The diameter of this cylinder will be 2.26 inches. The piece is bent by hand and then knocked into shape on the round mandrel.

To get the ends to meet now that the metal is work-hardened and springy from the pounding, I bend the ends of the metal over and under each other until they spring together. Before soldering the cylinder, I coat the entire piece with flux, as usual, inside and out. Again I use medium solder, which has a color very close to that of sterling itself. (Figure 13) The entire piece is then heated, with the temperature brought up evenly.

After the cylinder has been soldered together, it must be pounded into shape. This is done by placing it over the mandrel, forcing it onto the widest point, and pounding the metal with a rawhide mallet. (Figure 14) I work just along the outer edge and continually flip the piece over to keep it cylindrical.

The cylinder is now ready to be placed inside the frame of the

Figure 18. The piece is coated with yellow ocher.

Figure 19. When the posts are in position, they are filed down to a smooth finish.

Figure 20. The copper domes are cut out.

Figure 21. The domes are made with dapping tool and hammer.

bracelet to form the sleeve. Before soldering it into place I must flux the entire piece again. This time I use an easy solder, because it has a lower melting point than medium solder; if I were to reheat the piece to the temperature required for medium solder, the joints at the tips would reopen. I place small chips of easy solder along the inside of the cylinder, cutting them from strip solder. It is important to flux this chip solder too; if it's not fluxed, it won't flow.

Again the entire piece is heated. When the flux begins to turn glassy, I know I am at about 1100 degrees. Easy solder melts at 1270 degrees. When finished, the piece is again dropped into the pickle.

In order to give more depth to the piece, I add a piece of 16-gauge square wire to the perimeter of the cylinder. The wire is bent into shape and soldered together. I place the wire on the bracelet, fit it by hand, then flux and reheat the whole piece to the proper soldering temperature. Here again I use easy wire solder, since the joints are accessible. (Figure 15)

Next I want to place the posts in position on the outer sides of the bracelet. For these I cut short pieces of 16-gauge square wire. A careful filing job is necessary because a pressure fit is required. (Figure 16) Each side of the bracelet has five posts; there are fifteen in all. Five posts at a time are placed and then soldered. (Figure 17)

Figure 22. A ⅛-inch hole is drilled in each dome.

Figure 23. Bumps are added with a small chasing tool.

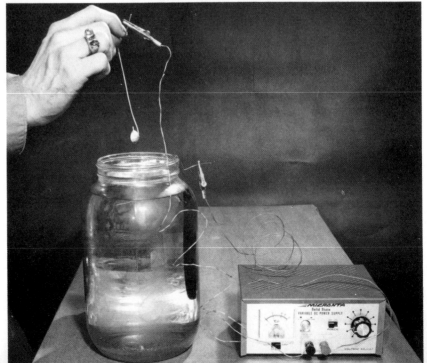

Figure 24. The beads are silverplated for seven or eight hours.

I then use yellow ocher, a solder flow inhibitor, for the first time. I use it because the posts are being soldered with easy solder, which has already been used on the cylinder. I want to save the lowest melting solder—extra-easy—for the next step, so I have to repeat the use of easy solder here. All the previously soldered joints are coated with yellow ocher, and easy solder is applied directly to the post joints, which have first been fluxed. (Figure 18)

Yellow ocher comes in a powder form and is mixed with water to the consistency of poster paint. When it is used, the piece should be rinsed clean before being dropped into the pickle, as the yellow ocher will cloud the solution (though it will not interfere with its effectiveness). After all three sides are soldered, all the posts are filed down. (Figure 19)

The remaining work on the bracelet involves placing a dome on each of the points. These domes will be done in a wood-grain style, a technique in which metal is given a surface decoration resembling wood.

The way this is done traditionally, as the Japanese developed it, is a complex process. A sheet of copper or bronze is sandwiched between two sheets of silver and all three are soldered together. They are then rolled through a mill or beaten with a hammer until they are taken down to the thickness of one sheet. As the beating increases the length of the piece, it is subsequently cut in half and soldered together again. The six-layered piece is then run through the mill or hammered again, and again reduced in size. It is cut in two and soldered once more, making twelve

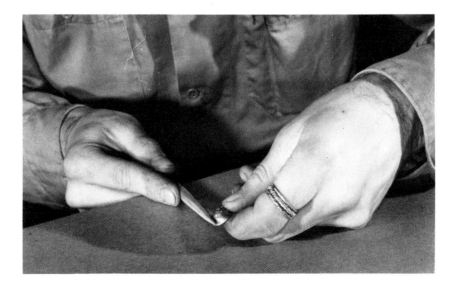

Figure 25. The bumps are filed down with a small file.

layers. The process is repeated until forty-eight layers or more of metal are soldered together. The more layers, the greater the detail.

Next, small bumps are pounded from the bottom side with a chasing tool. These bumps, in turn, are filed down to the level of the metal, leaving a beautiful wood-grain design on the surface of the material.

There is one big problem with this method: the repeated heating of the material causes air pockets to form, and when filing down the bumps, it is easy to hit an air pocket and leave a pit in the metal.

The new approach I am developing takes longer but avoids the problem of air pockets. It involves a series of electroplating operations. I begin with a matrix, a piece of inexpensive copper. I plate this metal with silver, in a silver cyanide solution at 1/20 ampere for about seven hours. Next, I plate it with copper, again for seven hours, and then with silver. A total of twelve platings is required for the piece.

The great advantage of this method is that it avoids air pockets; the plating is perfect, from one layer to the next. But it has other problems. The piece cannot be heated, for the plating will peel off. Also it is not possible to knock out the bumps with the chasing tool after the plating occurs, because the plating will crack. Therefore, the soldering and knocking out of bumps must be done before plating; the bumps can be filed down after the plating.

Electroplating is done with direct current (d.c.). Common household current has to pass through a rectifier and be converted into d.c., so that the electricity flows from the positive to the negative terminal. The art object goes on the negative pole; the positive pole takes a pure metal anode. If you are plating with silver, a silver anode is used; with copper, a copper anode. Also needed is a solution that can conduct both an electric current, called an electrolyte, and metallic ions from the positive to the negative pole.

In the case of silver I use a silver cyanide bath, which is commercially prepared. It is extremely dangerous and has to be used in an isolated area. The copper bath I mix myself, using twenty-four ounces of copper sulfate and six ounces of sulfuric acid per gallon of distilled water. *Under no circumstances should you allow the copper bath and the cyanide bath to come into contact with one another, as the contact produces cyanide gas.*

When I plate, I use a low amperage, because if I increase the current the plating won't be smooth. With a fast plating tiny beads appear on the surface. This type of buildup is called electroforming and cannot be used here.

Figure 26. Strips of bezel wire are joined with hard solder.

Figure 27. Perfect circles
are formed by pounding
wire into shape.

44

Figure 28. The bezel rims are soldered onto a silver sheet.

If you don't have a rectifier, two dry-cell batteries hooked up in series will do (with the positive pole of one battery hooked to the negative pole of the other). Two batteries in series have double the voltage of two separate batteries.

There are several things to be done before placing the copper piece in the first bath. First, a copper disk is made with the use of a hole punch. (Figure 20) Next, the copper piece is shaped into a dome with a dapping block and tool. The dapping block has different sizes of hemispheric depressions in it, and by forcing the metal disk into the desired depression with a dapping tool and hammer, a half dome is produced. (Figure 21)

Next I drill a $1/8$-inch hole in the top of each dome. (Figure 22) An opal is to be mounted in each of these holes. I then take the domes, or beads, and knock out bumps from the concave side with a small chasing tool. (Figure 23) The beads are then silverplated for seven or eight

Figure 29. Excess wire is cut away with jeweler's saw.

hours, at a low amperage. **(Figure 24)** Next I plate them in copper for the same length of time. This process continues until twelve layers have been built up, alternating between silver and copper and ending with a layer of silver.

When the process is completed, the beads are taken out of the baths and the bumps are filed off. **(Figure 25)** Now the half dome is smooth again, and the different layers of grain are exposed.

The file marks left from removing the bumps are removed by silicone carbide papers. I start with 220 grit, go on to 400 grit, and finally use 600 grit. Then I use a brass wire brush. Scratch brushing gives a burnished finish to the beads; it doesn't actually *scratch* them, but it does smooth the metal and bring it up to a semi-high gloss.

The next step is to take iron binding wire (about 24 gauge), wrap it around the base of one of the beads, and mark it for size. This determines the circumference of the base of the beads. The length of binding

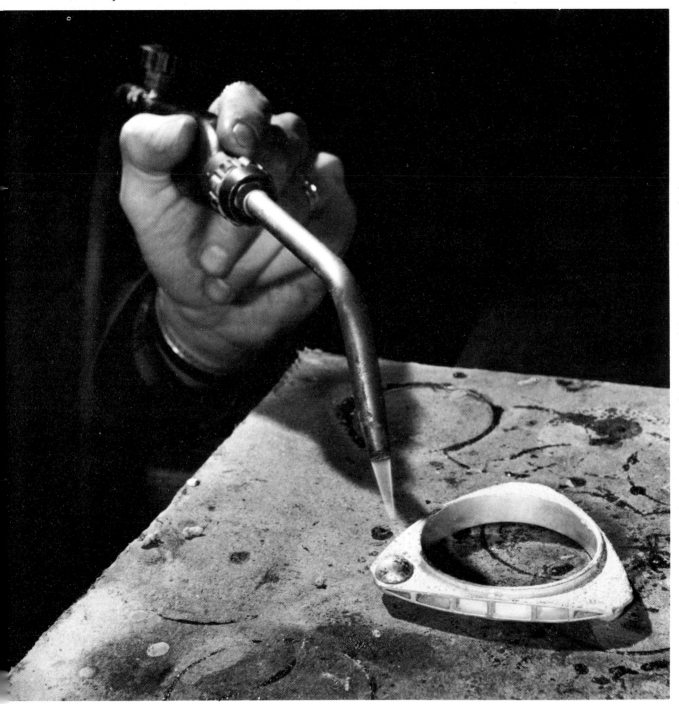

Figure 30. Domes are soldered to the bracelet near each point.

Figure 31. Hollow domes are intersected and soldered together.

wire is then laid on a strip of 28-gauge silver bezel wire. I cut three sections of silver, or bezel wire, to the length of the binding wire, bend them into circles, and solder them with hard solder. (Figure 26) Hard solder is used because it's a small mass of metal and it is easy to get it up to a high temperature—it melts somewhere around 1400 degrees. Then I knock the silver into perfect circles. (Figure 27) I now have circles that the beads will fit into.

These round rings of bezel wire are next laid on top of a silver sheet, and small chips of medium solder are placed around the insides. Everything is again fluxed, the rings are heated up to temperature, and

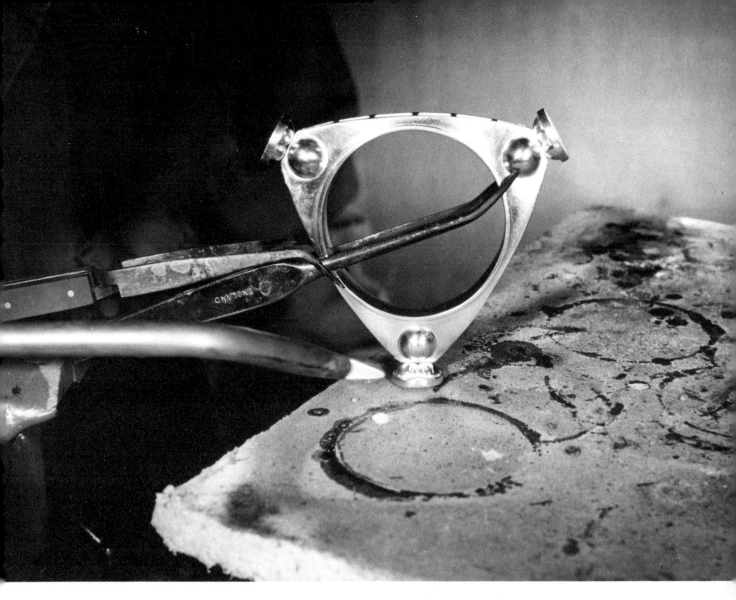

the wire is soldered onto the sheet. (Figure 28) I cut away the excess with a jeweler's saw. (Figure 29) What I end up with looks like a very squat cylinder with a base. The beads will be placed inside these cylinders.

Returning to the bracelet, I drill six holes near the points and solder six silver half domes, made with the dapping block and tool, over the holes. (Figure 30) The domes are hollow, and if I tried to solder them onto a flat sheet of metal, the gases inside the hollow would expand on heating and the solder would not completely seal. A hole in the metal, however, allows the gases to escape.

I next make and solder the platforms on which the wood-grain

Figure 32. The intersected domes form base platforms for the beads and are held in place with easy solder.

Figure 33. A burnisher is used to form the bezel around the beads.

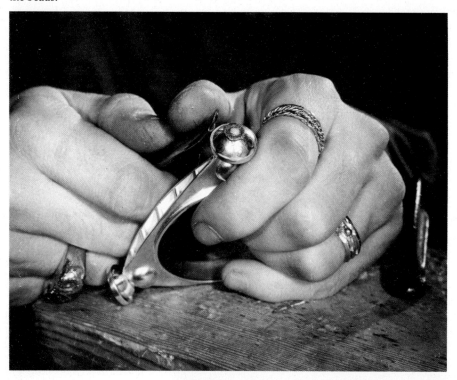

Figure 34. The hollow spaces on the sides are coated with liver of sulfur.

Figure 35. A brass wire brush will finish the piece in a semi-high gloss.

beads, sitting in their bezels, will be placed. I make six more smaller hollow domes, which are dapped out and which are partially intersected and soldered together, two at a time. (Figure 31) Then these two intersecting domes are soldered onto the bottom side of the metal base to which the bezels have been attached. Once again, a hole must be drilled in the base in order to let the gases escape. This is done to all three disks holding the bezels.

Now the entire unit is soldered onto the bracelet itself. (Figure 32) Small chips of extra-easy solder—the first time I use it on this piece—are placed at the contact points between the two intersecting domes and the points of the bracelet.

Next I electroform the opals themselves onto the wood-grain beads. (The beads are still separate from the bracelet.) I take the opals and, with a small amount of epoxy, set them into the $1/8$-inch holes in the top of each bead. I don't want the electroforming to take where I have done the wood-grain, so I protect the entire outside of the beads and the opals themselves with a coat of lacquer. To prepare the area where I want the electroforming to adhere I carefully paint a band of silver metallic paint around the base of the opal, making the section electrically conductive. Then I attach the wires that will feed the electricity to the beads, on the underside. The only parts that will take electroforming are the small area I've painted and the underside of the bead. These beads are electroformed only with copper.

Electroforming is done at a higher amperage, about $1/2$ ampere. It takes about two to three hours for each opal to be electroformed into place. The excess lacquer is then removed.

Finally everything is in place. The wood-grain beads with opals mounted in them are placed in the bezels; by using a burnisher, I push and smooth the bezels around the beads, which forms a strong enough grip to hold them in place. (Figure 33)

Then I electroform—in silver—a band around the bezel of the bracelet itself. The entire bracelet is painted with lacquer, and silver metallic paint is put just around the bezels. Then the bracelet is suspended in the silver bath and given $1/2$-ampere current for three to four hours to build up.

Liver of sulfur is then applied to the sides of the bracelet. (Figure 34) It darkens the silver and gives it a jet gray or black look. Finally, the piece is polished. I start polishing with 220 grit where needed, then with 400 grit, and finally with 600 grit. Then, last of all, using a brass wire brush, I bring the piece up to a final semi-high gloss. (Figure 35)

Gold Pendant. 18-karat gold, Australian opal; 3″ x 3″

53

Jew's Harp. 24-karat gold-plated sterling silver; 3″ x 4″

Necklace. Sterling silver and wood-grain style; 5″ x 6″

Spider Cage. Sterling silver cast and construction; 2¾″ x 2¾″ x 2¾″

Medal. Amber beads, ribbon, sterling silver; 2¾" x 5"

Silver Chalice. Sterling silver, fiddleback
maple, wild boar's tusk; 9" x 3"

Decorative Pocketknife
Gary Noffke

Gary Noffke, one of the outstanding craftsmen working in metals today, has a unique style that marks all his pieces. His work shows strength, an imaginative use of materials, and a wonderful sense of humor. There is nothing precious about his objects; they are bold statements that are skillfully crafted. The pocketknife he makes here is a good example of an object that is both useful and decorative and that can be made from an unlikely combination of materials.

Gary Noffke was born in Decatur, Illinois. He received the B.S. and M.S. degrees from Eastern Illinois University in Charleston and an M.F.A. degree from Southern Illinois University in Carbondale.

His work has been exhibited at the University of Georgia in Athens, 1970; the Inter D-2 Crafts Open Exhibition in the United States and Mexico; the Mount Allen International Museum in Mount Allen, Texas, 1971; the Metal '72 Invitational at the State University of New York at Brockport and the National Jewelry and Holloware Exhibition at Northern Illinois University in DeKalb, 1972; Objects for Preparing Food at the Museum of Contemporary Crafts in New York and the Renwick Gallery of the Smithsonian Institution in Washington, D.C., and Objects U.S.A., the National Crafts Invitational, at Kent State University in Kent, Ohio, 1973; the American Metalsmith Exhibition at the DeCordova Museum in Lincoln, Massachusetts, the First World Crafts Exhibition at the Ontario Science Centre in Toronto, and Goldsmith '74 at the Renwick Gallery and the Minnesota Museum of Art in Saint Paul, 1974.

His work is in the collections of the Mint Museum of Art in Charlotte, North Carolina; Southern Illinois University; and the National Collection of Fine Arts, Smithsonian Institution, Washington, D.C.

He is a member of the Society of North American Goldsmiths.

Gary Noffke has taught at Southern Illinois University; Stetson University, Deland, Florida; California State College of Los Angeles; the University of Georgia, Athens; and Penland School of Crafts. He lives in Farmington, Georgia.

Decorative Pocketknife. Carbon steel, silver, 18-karat gold

A pocketknife is a good object to make. It can be as decorative as a piece of jewelry, but strong enough to use as a tool. I make this small, decorative pocketknife from a flat, carbon steel bastard file. A file is naturally hard and tempered; in order to work with it successfully, to cut it into shape for the knife, I must first anneal it.

Annealing is a heating process that softens the steel so that it can be cut with another steel tool. Once it's in the shape I want, I just reharden and retemper the steel. For both the spring and the blade of the knife, I need just the one file, cut into two pieces.

Both annealing and hardening a piece of steel requires heating the steel to the same temperature. The difference is only in the cooling. To anneal the piece, I use a Prest-o-lite torch. (Figure 1) I heat the steel to a bright red glow (Figure 2), then, in a pumice pan, cover the steel with lump pumice, which will cause the steel to cool very slowly. Other materials, such as vermiculite, may be used as insulation, too. To harden the steel, again heat the metal with a torch to a bright red glow, but this time, quickly douse it in water.

For best results use the kiln to anneal. Take the metal up in a small electric kiln to 1425 degrees, which will give it a bright red color, then let it cool gradually in the normal cycle of the kiln. It usually takes two to three hours for a small piece to cool properly. To heat with a torch, the process I'm using, takes about half an hour.

Another test of temperature—either to anneal or harden—is to use a magnet. When the metal is no longer attracted to the magnet, you know the correct temperature has been reached.

For the handle of the knife I could use bone, ivory, amber, wood, plastic, or a combination of these materials over a metal frame. But for this piece I am going to use 14-gauge sterling silver, which will be cut into shape and fastened to the spring and blade with rivets. Later, on the silver handle, I'll do decorative work. The silver will serve as both the mechanical frame and the finished handle. If I used another handle material, I would rivet it to the top of the metal frame.

After the steel file has been annealed, I file the teeth off with a large, coarse-cut file. (Figure 3) This is a dramatic illustration of the effects of annealing, or of hardening and tempering carbon steel. It is also an accurate test of the steel's condition. If the hard-tempered file cuts into the steel easily, the steel is annealed.

The next step is to saw the spring and blade from the annealed file. I have made a sketch, very rough, of what I want, and I draw that on the metal. (Figure 4) Making preliminary sketches of my projects is

Figure 1. The steel file is annealed with a Prest-o-lite torch.

Figure 2. A pumice pan is used for annealing.

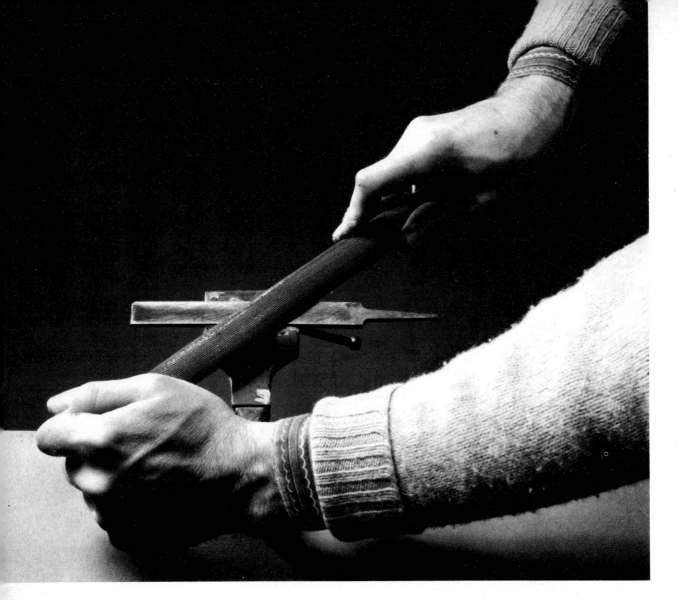

Figure 3. The file teeth are removed with a large, coarse-cut file.

important to me, but I like to see the form itself evolve from the working process. The piece should not be completely determined by a sketch, which is a craft of another medium; trying to copy a sketch, no matter what the technique, almost always denies the natural qualities of the metal. It generally makes the object seem sterile, though that would naturally depend on the skill and knowledge of the artist involved.

In sawing, the important thing is not to hurry! Hurrying puts too much pressure on the blade. Always keep the frame of the jeweler's saw as vertical as possible, and the blade tight. (Figure 5) It's also important to hold the work steady.

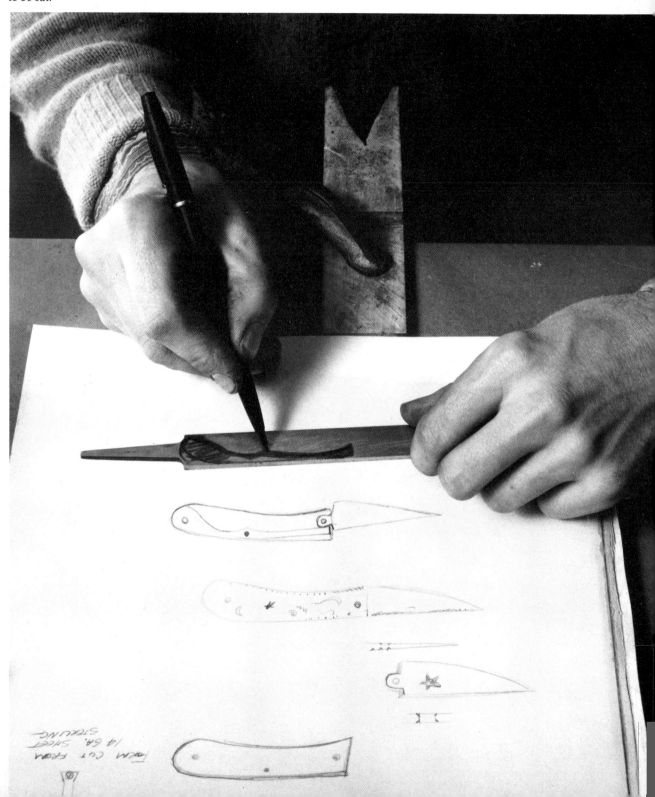

Figure 4. A sketch is drawn directly on the metal that is to be cut.

Figure 5. The saw should
be kept vertical and the
blade tight.

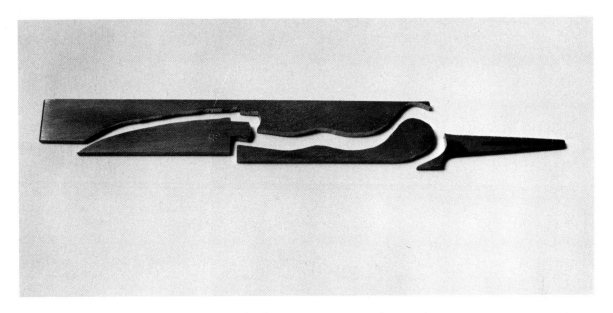

Figure 6. Two pieces of the knife are cut from one file.

The thickness of the spring, or backpiece, is very important. At the point where it's riveted in the center of the spring and where it touches, the curved part on the back of the blade should be fairly even and gradually tapered. The spring has to be a precise thickness in order to work well. If it's too thick, the knife will be hard to open; if too thin, the blade will be loose.

I have cut the pieces larger than I want, which leaves room for refinement and variation in the form. (Figure 6) I grind the blade down and taper it to a point. This can be done by filing, but filing takes longer. The final forming of the blade, however, is done with a file, which allows for a more precise shape.

Once the blade and spring (or backpiece) have been shaped, I drill holes for the rivets, then decorate the blade. All the forming and finishing of the metal is done while the steel is annealed. Afterward, it is rehardened and tempered.

Drilling the steel is a very critical part of making the pocketknife. The holes must be exact or the knife will not function properly. The rivet hole in the blade doesn't go in the center of the pivot section. It is placed slightly toward the point of the blade, so that the blade, when it turns, exerts the most pressure against the spring. It will snap shut and hold tight. It is very important to have the pivot point shaped properly—straight on top, slightly slanted at the bottom, and curved in the back. If the bottom of the pivot point is slightly slanted it will act as a stop for

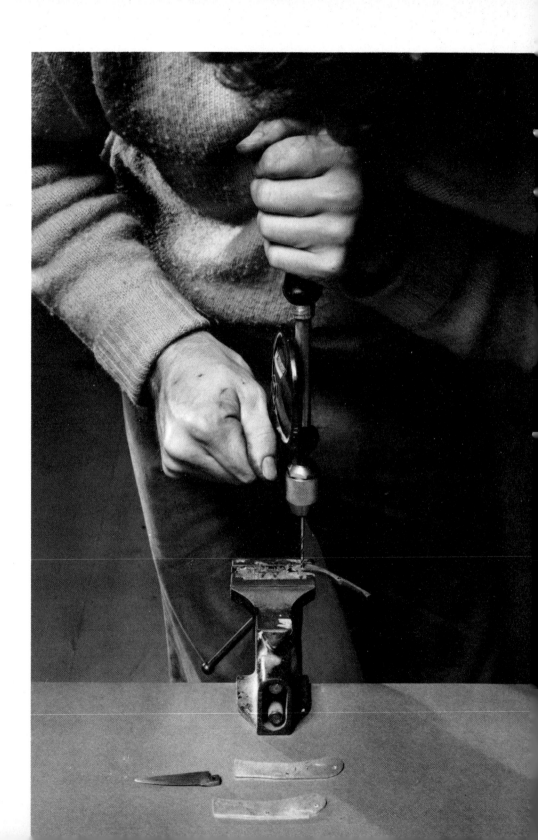

Figure 7. The holes are drilled before the piece is filed down. Allow room for error.

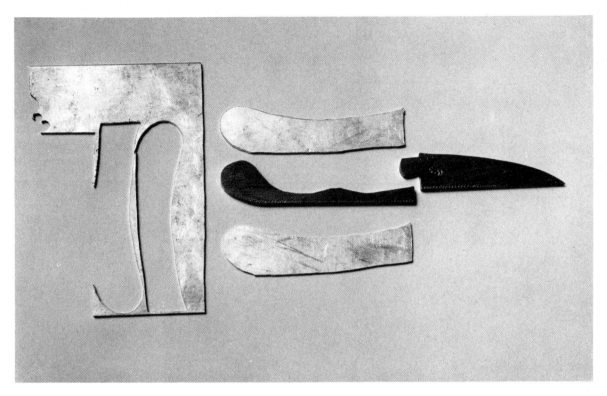

the blade when it is shut and will keep the edge off the hard steel spring. It gives the blade a fixed place to set.

Figure 8. Room is left on the cut out frame pieces for more forming.

Before drilling, I cut a hole in the steel with a small ball burr in a flexible shaft. The position of this hole is most critical. Once the hole is made I can drill without having the bit slip. In drilling the steel I use a drill the same size as the wire I'm going to use to make the rivets. I also use a drill press, because the hole must be drilled straight through in order for the blade to open correctly.

The center section, where the spring flexes, should be drilled before it is completely filed down. I use a size 40 bit in the middle and a size 35 bit at the end. I want to be able to use as large a rivet as possible. (Figure 7) It is important, too, not to place the hole too close to the edge of the steel, especially if a material like bone or wood will be attached to the frame. It certainly shouldn't be closer than 1/16 inch.

In making the spring holes, clamp the spring in place on the silver frame with a hand clamp, then drill the holes in the silver frame by first drilling through the steel. This will guarantee that the holes are correctly placed. The frame holds the two pieces—spring and blade—together and is fixed to the spring in two places; it is fixed to the blade in only one place. Mechanically, this knife is a simple object.

The frame is made from two pieces of 14-gauge silver. I cut out the form from a preliminary sketch, leaving room for more forming later. (Figure 8) This frame or handle could be made of thicker material but weight is a problem. For a small knife such as this one, the 14-gauge silver frame provides a thick enough handle.

After all the rivet holes are drilled in the spring and blade, I complete the surface treatment of the steel before I reharden and temper it.

For the surface work on the steel I use only a flexible shaft machine with small round dental burrs. There are special burrs made for this machine, but they're too long for me to control. They could, though, be cut down in length if dental burrs are not available.

I place the blade on a leather bag filled with lead shot and, using both hands, work the flexible shaft over the blade. (Figure 9) It's important that only one hand be used to hold the handpiece of the machine, leaving at least one finger or the thumb of the other hand free to hold the blade in position. It is a tough and demanding job. With this machine a variety of lines can be cut into the metal; it can also be used as a carving tool. I tend to work with small designs or decorative elements, which is generally somewhat easier than controlling long flowing lines.

Now it is necessary to reinforce the section of the frame where the blade is riveted. I will use 18-karat yellow gold in this case. It will provide another color, as well as an accent or design element for the knife.

I forge out a piece of 18-gauge gold and take it down to 20-gauge. I thin it out by placing the metal on an anvil and striking it with a cross peen hammer. The cross peen hammer moves the metal in only one direction, and that is what I want in this particular operation.

I generally don't have on hand all the gauges of metals I need for a project, especially gold, but that has advantages. It gets me involved in working the metal itself instead of just going to a drawer and pulling out a piece of metal and sawing it to size. When I take the trouble to shape the metal and work with it, there is more of a human element, more of me, in the production of the piece. I feel closer to the finished product.

I have cut the frame to fit the spring and the blade, and I have now cut the gold. Gold is a strong metal and I want to place it at the end of the frame, where the blade rivet goes. This is done by sweat soldering.

When soldering silver to gold I generally use silver solder. Both pieces must be perfectly flat, with no gaps! First I cut small paillons (or chips) of silver solder from a 24-gauge sheet and arrange them on the

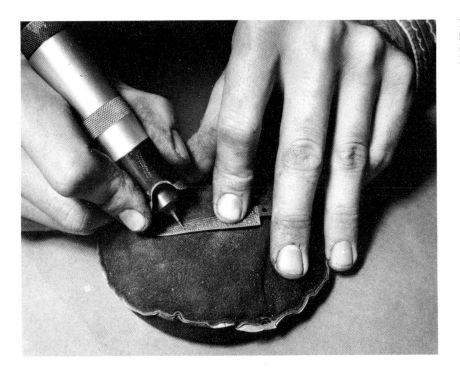

Figure 9. Surface work is done with a flexible shaft, working on a small lead-shot leather bag.

Figure 10. Paillons are cut from 24-gauge silver sheets.

backs of the pieces I'm going to solder. I flux the metal and the paillons and melt them on the gold. (Figure 10) When sweat soldering I don't have to worry about the solder jumping around or getting on the edges.

After the paillons are sweat-soldered, I again flux them and arrange the two pieces of gold on the silver. I use paste flux because it doesn't burn off quickly. To clean off the flux after soldering, I just drop the piece into acid. Sparex is what I use; it's safe and simple.

When I am ready to fix the gold pieces onto the silver handle of the knife, I flux the whole piece once more and heat the object from below. (Figure 11) I have also used small paillons of gold solder in other places on the knife, for color contrast and decoration. Once the soldering is done I drop the whole piece back into the acid to be cleaned.

Then, before the knife is riveted together, I use stamps, chisels, and chasing tools on the surface of the frame. I've made the stamps out of tool steel, and cut, filed, and chiseled different designs onto the faces; the stamps are hard-tempered and I use them with a hammer, working on a surface plate. (Figure 12) Any number of images and textures can be obtained with these tools. But the work has to be done before the piece is assembled, because the silver must be supported by a surface plate or anvil. (Figure 13) Other techniques, such as engraving, carving with a

Figure 11. The object is heated from above and below, after the piece has been fluxed.

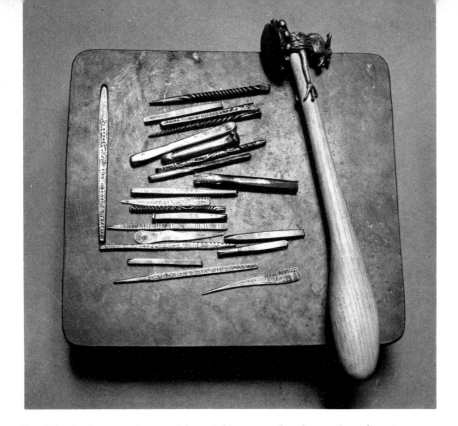

Figure 12. An assortment of chasing tools.

flexible shaft, scraping, and burnishing, can be done after the pieces are riveted together.

The blade and spring must be hardened, too, before the pieces are riveted together. This is a two-step process. First, I harden as explained earlier. (If the form of the blade allows, harden only the edge. One-eighth of an inch up from the cutting edge is sufficient.) The blade is heated slowly and evenly, with the torch being concentrated on the thick, back side of the blade. Overheating the point and edge should be avoided. The entire edge should arrive at a straw-colored heat at the same time, at which point the blade is quenched in water immediately. Then I finish the steel with abrasive paper, removing the heat oxidation that has occurred in hardening.

In tempering, the straw color appears first at a lower heat, then the red, and then blue. To become familiar with these colors take a small piece of steel, clean it with abrasive paper, and then heat it at one point until it turns straw and red and blue. The colors are also indicative of the rate at which steel conducts heat.

In tempering, too, the lower the temperature of the steel when quenched, the harder it will be—also the more brittle. The higher the temperature, the softer the metal becomes. The spring in the knife should

Figure 13. Work with chasing tools must be done before the piece is assembled, because the silver must be supported by the surface plate.

be tempered at a blue heat. At this temper it will have the proper strength and flexibility.

The next step is drilling holes in the frame for all the rivets. The drilling must be exact, with all holes in perfect alignment. To drill them properly, clamp the spring in its place to one side of the frame and drill through the established holes in the spring and the frame. Then clamp the two sides of the frame together and drill through the already established holes and then through the other side of the frame. This will ensure that all parts are aligned.

Drilling the front of the frame where the blade is riveted requires much care. First, fix the spring temporarily to one side of the frame, using the appropriate size wires in the rivet holes. Then put the blade

Figure 14. A small ball peen hammer is used to spread the rivet heads.

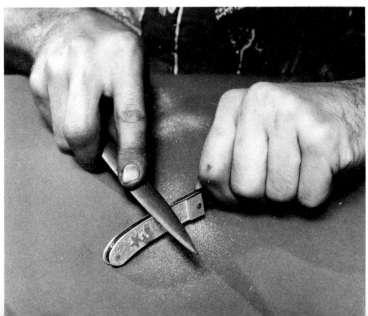

Figure 15. The frame is filed down with coarse and then with fine files.

in place and mark the center of its rivet hole on the frame. Then raise that point toward the top edge of the frame—about 1/16 inch—and drill. This will ensure that there will be tension on the blade from the spring at all times, which is necessary if the blade is to snap open and closed. Next place both sides of the frame together, clamp, and drill the second side of the frame.

The next step is riveting the finished spring and blade to the frame. The holes drilled in the frame are tapered on the outside, so that when the ends of the rivet wires are spread they are mechanically trapped. A flexible shaft, file, or tapered reamer may be used to taper.

I use silver rivets to fix the spring to the frame and mild steel (cut from a nail) to fix the blade to the frame. The rivets should extend through the frame on each side for about two-thirds of their own diameter. In spreading the rivet heads, I use a small ball peen hammer, working each end evenly, turning the piece often, and always supporting its back side with a steel plate or anvil. (Figure 14) I concentrate the hammering on the center of each rivet. This keeps the rivet both from bending and from having thin edges. The rivet wires should fit tightly in the drilled holes before they are hammered. If they are too small, they tend to bend instead of spreading evenly on the heads.

Care should be taken not to set the rivet that holds the blade too tightly. If it is hammered down too much, there will be a great deal of friction between the blade and the frame and the blade will not snap open and closed. When all the rivets are set, they may either be filed flush to the frame or left exposed for added strength or decoration. On this knife I leave them exposed for both reasons.

It's better to do the final finishing after the piece has been riveted together. To file the frame down to the spring, begin with a coarse-cut file, then switch to a fine file. (Figure 15) After filing, I use a scraper to remove most file marks, and then I use a burnisher for the final finish. Using a hand burnisher adds another element to the surface texture. Machine buffs with compounds tend to remove surface information, but they are useful if a highly polished surface is desired.

The last step is sharpening the blade. For this I use a coarse and medium Carborundum stone, then a hard Arkansas stone. To stone the blade, direct the edge of the blade, at the desired angle, into the stone. The smaller the angle between the blade and the stone, the sharper the edge will be, but also the thinner and weaker. A 20-percent angle, approximately, will give a good sharp and strong edge.

With the sharpening of the blade, the pocketknife is completed.

Mother's Perfume Bottle. Cast 18-karat yellow gold bottle with chased surface, forged and chased 14-karat yellow gold chain

Fritz's Beads
Assorted materials and techniques
from and for commemorative
occasions

Medal of Honor
Pierced steel with carved
surface and decorative
silver rivets

Casey's Ring
Pierced, cast, and fabricated
sterling, 18-karat
yellow gold, mild steel

Penland Torso
Arline M. Fisch

Arline M. Fisch is internationally known for her large-size body jewelry. Her work incorporates most of the traditional jewelry techniques, but she recently has been working in weaving techniques that she has applied to metals.

Arline M. Fisch was born in New York City. She received a B.S. in Art from Skidmore College, Saratoga Springs, New York, and an M.A. in Art from the University of Illinois, Urbana. In addition she studied at the School of Arts and Crafts and the Bernhard Hertz Guldvaerefabrik in Copenhagen, Denmark.

Her work has been shown at a great number of art and crafts exhibitions, both in the United States and abroad. She has had solo exhibitions at the Pasadena Museum of Art, 1962; the Wooden Horse Gallery in Laguna Beach, California, 1965; the Museum of Decorative Arts in Copenhagen, 1967; Museum West in San Francisco and the Museum of Contemporary Crafts in New York, 1968; The Egg and Eye in Los Angeles, 1969; the Gallery in Denver, 1970; Goldsmiths' Hall in London and Lee Nordness Galleries in New York, 1971; and The Slocumb Gallery in Johnson City, Tennessee, 1973.

Her work is in the collections of the Minnesota Museum of Art in Saint Paul; the Worshipful Company of Goldsmiths in London; The Johnson Wax Collection (Objects: USA); Western Illinois University in Macomb; and numerous private collections in the United States and Europe.

She is a member of the Society of North American Goldsmiths.

Arline Fisch has taught at Wheaton College; Skidmore College; San Diego State College; Haystack Mountain School of Crafts, Deer Isle, Maine; the School of Arts and Crafts in Copenhagen; and Penland School of Crafts. She lives in San Diego, California.

Pendant-brooch, "Penland Torso." Sterling silver, fine silver, *millefiore* glass, removable silver chain; 6" high x 6" wide

I was born and brought up in New York City, which I consider one of the great advantages of my life. I was exposed at a very early age to all the wonders of New York—museums, theater, music, dance, art, and architecture. During my high school years, I spent every Saturday in Manhattan working on a museum assignment, going to a theater or ballet matinee, or just walking around enjoying the environment. I have never lost my taste for such urban delights, and I still enjoy strolling through city streets looking at the peole, the buildings, and the shop windows. As time goes by, I realize how much I absorbed of the history of art and architecture and of images and ideas from that urban experience. The high school I went to was rather large, about five thousand students, and it had a very good art program, so I majored in art. The program was primarily painting and commercial art. Most of my fellow students were gearing themselves to go to Pratt Institute, which was considered the ultimate goal. If you got into Pratt with your portfolio, you had made it! I was rather a perverse individual and did not want to go to Pratt and definitely did not want to be a commercial artist.

I chose to go to Skidmore instead because it was a liberal arts college, small, all women, but with a very strong art department. The art program was excellent, with a sound education in design. I majored in art education, but I did more painting than anything else. Curiously, I did very little in the crafts and nothing in jewelry or metalwork. I did study art history in some depth, which was a continuation of my interests and experience as a high school student. I also became fascinated by the social history of art, the study of which filled in some of the gaps in my education.

I decided I wanted to teach at the college level, which meant that I needed an advanced degree. I was eager to go to graduate school for another reason—I had not yet made a commitment to any particular area of art. I was floating around, doing lots of things and enjoying them all, but not feeling any serious commitment to a particular direction. I started graduate school with the idea of majoring in painting and discovered after a semester at the University of Illinois that it really wasn't what I should be doing. I had the fortune (or misfortune) to share classes with students who were G.I. veterans, who had gone through a whole lifetime of experiences that they were able to express visually. They were so far in advance of anything I was capable of either feeling or doing that I could see it was simply not for me, at least not at that time in my life. I switched to crafts and worked in ceramics, which I disliked rather intensely, and in metal, which I discovered that I liked rather well, though I had had no

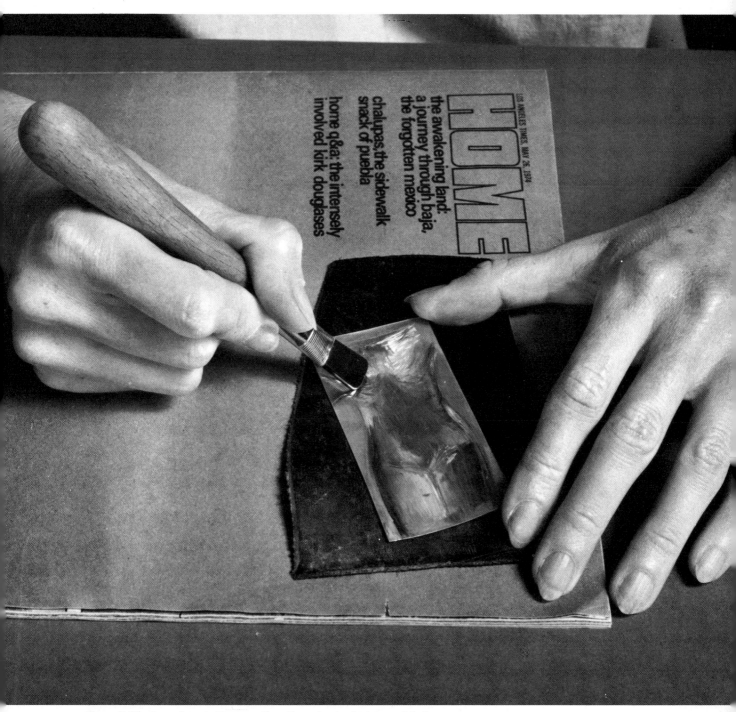

Figure 1. The torso form is 30-gauge fine silver sheet, which is modeled or repousséd from the back, using a burnisher. The metal rests on a soft pad of leather and newspaper that responds to even the slightest pressure of the tool. In this case a hematite burnisher is used, but it could as well be steel or even wood.

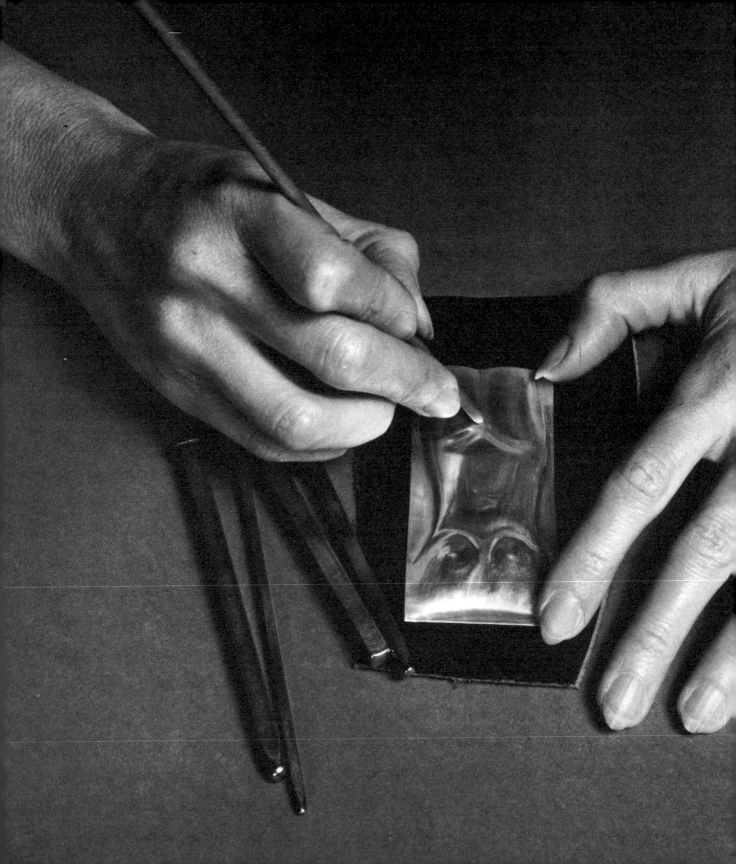

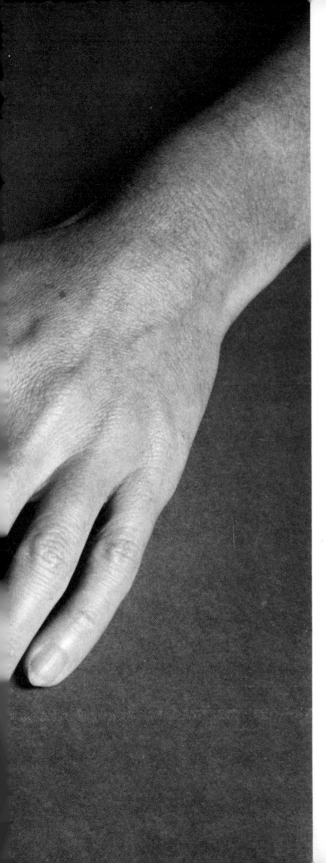

Figure 2. The torso is detailed and given added dimension by working from the front with a wooden rod. The fine silver hardens from the constant pressure of the burnisher, so it has been annealed once during the modeling.

Figure 3. The wings and pedestal are a single element cut from a sheet of 20-gauge sterling silver. An accurate paper pattern has been glued directly to the metal to guide in sawing out the form.

previous experience in that material. I spent a year and a half in metal-work, and when I finished my degree, I was hired by Wheaton College in Massachusetts—again, a women's liberal arts school with a small art department. I taught there for two years, and although my teaching assignment was in design, drawing, and painting, that period really determined my being a jeweler.

Wheaton is located near Attleboro and Taunton, Massachusetts, which are the centers for the American commercial jewelry trade. Many large companies had factories in the area that produced both jewelry and flatware. The school had no facilities for me to do anything of my own, but rather than set up my own studio, I went looking for a place to work. I found a jewelry studio that belonged to a man who worked in one of the factories during the day and did a little repair work at night. He was

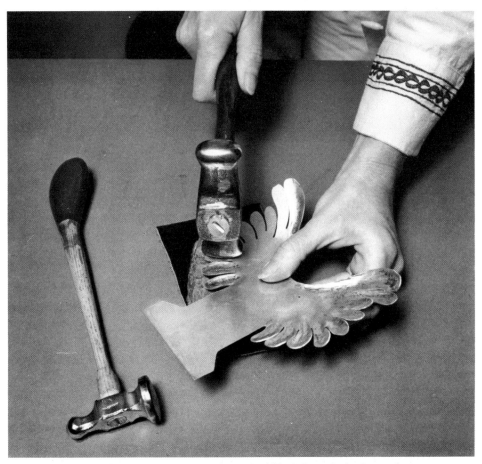

Figure 4. The wings are hammered on a lead block from the back in order to give them a three-dimensional quality. Grooves have first been made in the block with a hammer so that it acts as a die in shaping the feathers.

a terribly nice man, with a funny little shop full of tools and machines and bits and pieces of commercial jewelry. He gave me a key so that I could come and go as I wished, and I worked every night at the studio after teaching during the day. There's not much to do in Norton, Massachusetts, so I worked a great deal! After two years, I arrived at several serious conclusions: one, I had to leave where I was teaching because it was too stifling; and, two, I very much needed more technical training if I was to develop as a jeweler.

I applied for a Fulbright to go to Denmark, because at that time Scandinavian design in silver was considered the best in the modern world. I received the grant to study at the School of Arts and Crafts in Copenhagen. That was a rather harrowing experience at first, because the director didn't really want Americans in his school. However, a little pressure from the Fulbright office in Denmark got me into the school on the condition that I could understand and speak Danish! I remember being called into the director's office on the first day of school, having him tell me that I was only there to pick the brains and steal the ideas of the Danes, and then to go home and set myself up to compete with their market. I assured him that that wasn't my interest; that I had my own ideas and that I really only wanted someone to help me learn how to make what was in my own head. He didn't believe me at the time. However, at the end of the year (during which time I worked very hard) he apologized and said that he had been very pleased with my performance. Subsequently, other people were able to go to the same school under similar grants and under the same conditions.

I did find that the school was not exactly what I needed. The Danish system of education for jewelers is to train people as apprentices in a workshop for four or five years, after which time they take an examination. The top ten apprentices in the country are then invited to attend the Goldsmiths' School for a two-year period of intensive design training. My fellow students already knew how to make everything, but they had had no design training, and so the emphasis of the program was on design and drawing with some instruction in metallurgy and gemmology. Only a limited amount of time was given to actual workshops in specialized areas like enameling and smithing. It was a real conflict for me. I wanted to be in that school because I felt I needed to be with other people to share ideas, and yet to sit for a whole afternoon drawing and rendering jewelry was not why I had come to Denmark.

After several months of frustration, I met one of the directors of the school, who arranged for me to work in a commercial workshop. I was

Figure 5. After annealing, the feathers are planished from the front with a small, highly polished hammer. This process both refines the form and provides a delicate surface texture that will be retained in the finished piece.

seated next to a young person who spoke some English and who was instructed to help me with making my own pieces. I didn't want to (and couldn't) work as an apprentice on the commercial pieces they were making, but I did want to acquire as much technical skill as possible. I arranged my program with the director of the workshop to include experiences in many areas—stone setting, casting, enameling. I worked there every afternoon for the remainder of the year. I still attended the silversmithing class at the school to keep in touch with the students, and was fortunate enough to be invited to share several wonderful trips with the school to various parts of Europe. That alone made my year overseas! I worked every day, starting at the school at 8:00 A.M., spending my afternoons working on my own pieces at the workshop, then studying the Danish language at night. It was a difficult but very productive year, and I learned a great deal from the Danes.

I was given the opportunity to stay in Denmark a second year on a renewal of my Fulbright grant, but I chose instead to accept a job teaching at Skidmore College. I needed to get away from the Danish influence, which was very compelling—the idea that everything had to be perfect in design and technique, that only precious materials, properly treated, constitute real jewelry, and that everything had to be suitable for millions of anonymous people. I didn't basically agree with those ideas, but I needed time and experience to develop my own alternatives.

It was a good thing for me to leave Denmark at that point. When I went to Skidmore, I set up my own workshop right away and began working consistently in jewelry, striving to find my own artistic identity, a goal I continue to pursue. At Skidmore, I taught basic design classes and some art education, rather than jewelry. When I was asked to teach weaving, I said I couldn't because I didn't know how, but I would like to learn. I was sent on a Danforth Grant for a six-week session at Haystack, where I studied with Jack Lenor Larsen and Ted Hallman. It was a marvelous experience and I enjoyed the opportunity of working in a totally different medium. I became deeply involved in the historical aspects of weaving, particularly pre-Columbian textiles. In fact, I became so fascinated that I went to South America in 1963 to look at ancient textiles and metalwork. I suppose that was the beginning of my interest in combining those two technologies, because in looking at pre-Columbian artifacts, I could see that metal and textiles were frequently used together in very interesting ways.

I stayed at Skidmore four years and left reluctantly, for Saratoga Springs is a beautiful place in both summer and winter. However, I felt it

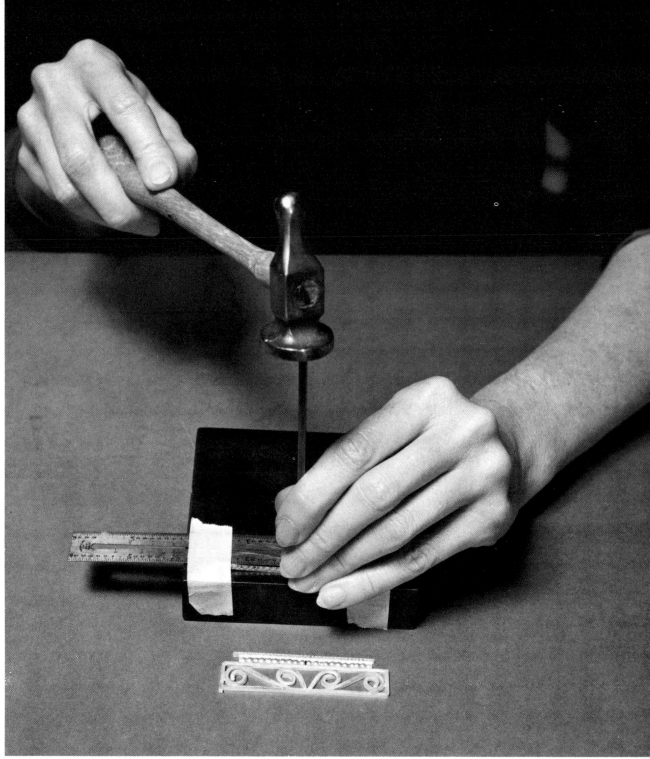

Figure 6. A decorative element for the pedestal area is composed and assembled separately. Square wire is used for the frame and scrollwork, with further ornamentation chased into wire and sheet-metal strips. The whole panel is soldered on a charcoal block with hard solder, and then cleaned and filed on the back before being placed on the main body of the pendant.

Figure 7. The decorative panel is soldered into position using medium solder.

was time for a change. I had never been to the West Coast, so I took a job in San Diego teaching jewelry and weaving, and I have been there off and on ever since. Off and on because I've taken several years off from teaching on various grants to travel and to live and work in Denmark.

I've always traveled a great deal and find that it is the most stimulating and mind-expanding thing I can do. My idea of traveling is to go someplace where there is something I want to see and to work hard at looking and understanding. When I lived in Copenhagen, I was able to travel to Egypt for several weeks. That was the most fantastic experience, not just to be in the museums in Cairo, but to spend a week in Luxor

Figure 8. The torso panel will be mounted from the back and held in position with a series of silver rivets. The hole cut to receive the torso must fit exactly if the thin sheet is to be properly mounted and protected. Minor adjustments are carefully marked and filed for proper alignment.

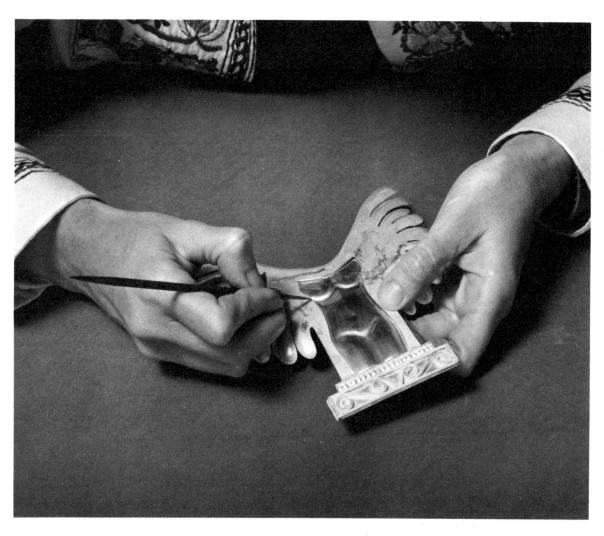

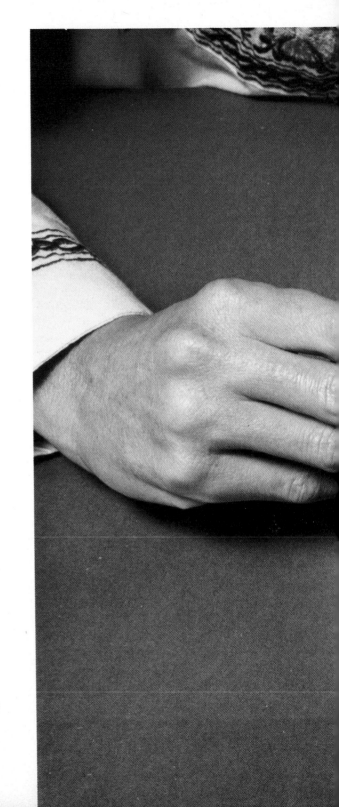

Figure 9. The *millefiore* glass slabs, which have been polished on lapidary equipment, are to be set as stones. A fine silver strip is cut and shaped to each piece of glass to serve as a bezel setting.

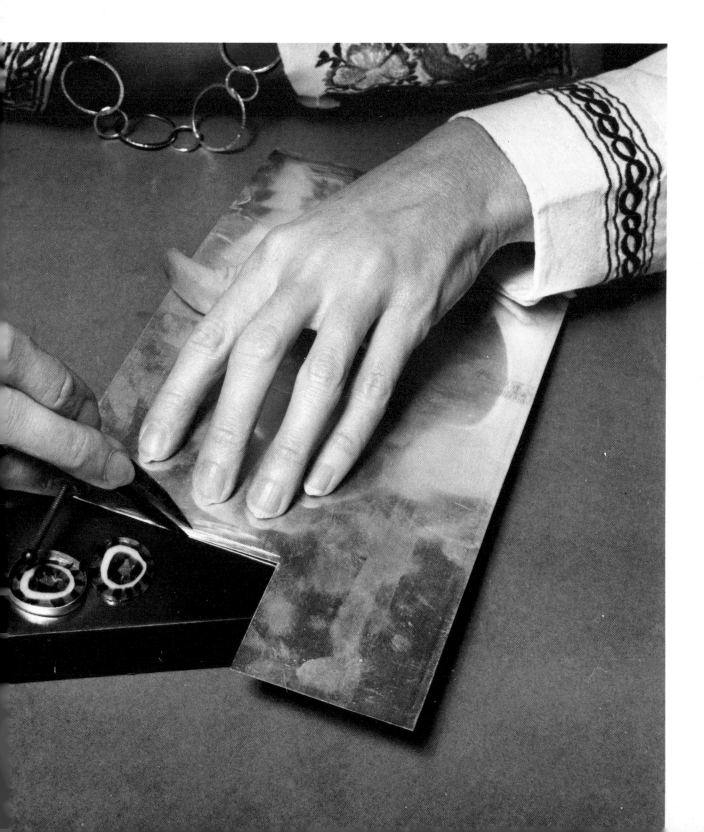

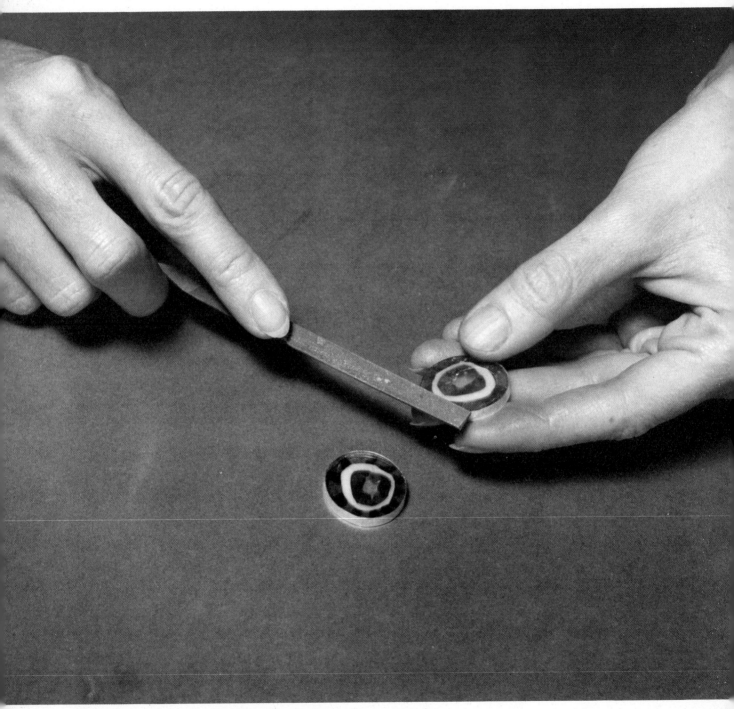

Figure 10. The shaped strips are soldered to a base plate of 24-gauge sterling silver. The strips are then filed down to the appropriate level for setting, before the whole unit is soldered into position on the wings.

and be totally surrounded by an ancient culture. I've done the same in Morocco, in Greece, in Turkey, and in South America, although there I stayed longer and moved through several countries and cultures.

My work is very involved with other cultures. I would say that since I made my break with Scandinavian modern, which I did when I returned from Denmark the first time, I am rarely influenced by contemporary work. I enjoy it and I am interested in what other people are doing, but my own work is not conditioned by it. I am much more influenced by other cultures, many of which I've studied in some detail. I have looked at ancient Egyptian jewelry extensively, and I've probably seen almost every piece in the public domain. But I am also very interested in the jewelry of Mongolia (of which there is a very large collection in Copenhagen), of the Arctic peoples, of the African peoples. I became very interested in Scythian work, and I went to Leningrad specifically to see the gold collection there. My travels are almost always determined by what I want to see, and my work is very much conditioned by what I do see. I draw constantly while I travel, accurately and in detail. I spend a long time studying a piece and, by drawing, I remember. Drawing has probably been the greatest learning experience I've had, technically as well as esthetically.

My work evolves out of what I have seen and what I have drawn, sometimes very specifically and sometimes in a general way. I have on occasion made pieces based on very specific objects that I've seen and was curious about or to which I reacted strongly. I don't feel that it is a bad thing to do; the piece becomes mine, in any case, because I'm not capable of copying anything directly. Most often, however, I tend to mix up what I've seen or studied, so that it is difficult to tell what a finished piece actually is based on. In fact, the images and ideas are so completely absorbed that they become part of my own design vocabulary.

There are several themes or motifs that I've used rather consistently for the past ten years. Wings and faces are the two images that recur time and again. I've done a great many pieces using wing forms, either birds or insects. It all started when I studied butterflies and made, in fact, a real butterfly piece just because I was so impressed by the delicacy of design. Since then the wings have become more and more abstract, that is, further and further away from real objects. They are simply winged forms, and I find myself using them frequently. In the same way, I continue to use the face image because it is expressive and imparts a particular mood, character, and personality to a piece.

I think I have a very nontechnical mind, because I'm not very con-

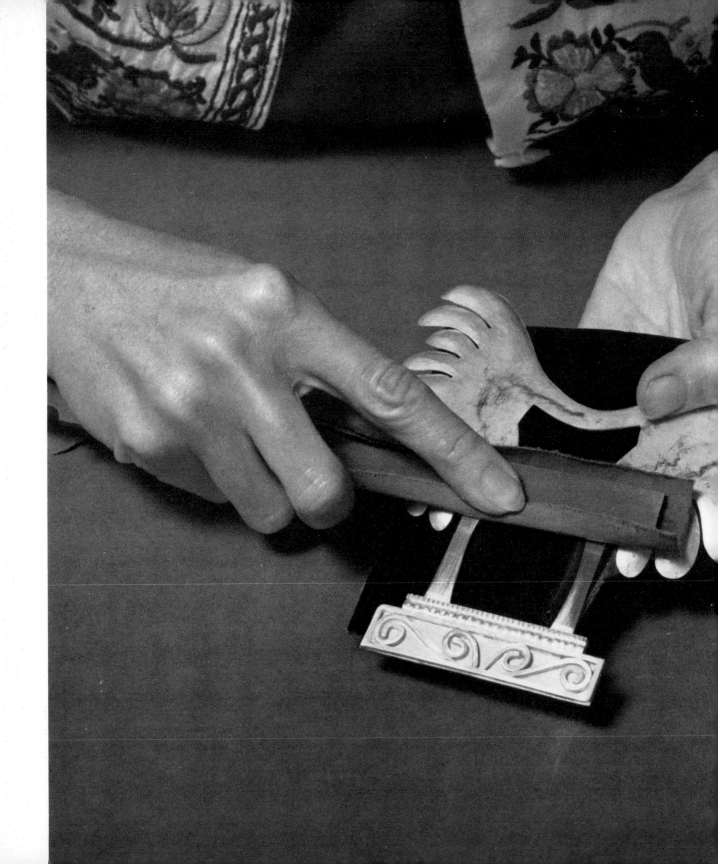

Figure 11. The whole piece will be finished and polished with a series of hand operations. First, all major scratches are removed with emery paper of a medium grit, followed by a thorough Scotch stoning to remove blemishes.

Figure 12. The surface is further refined by hand rubbing with very fine 600 emery paper. Since the final finish will be a soft one, the piece is heated, cooled, and pickled several times after the surface has been polished. This process builds up a deposit of fine silver on the surface, which will be burnished with a brass wire brush in the textured areas and lightly buffed with rouge in the smooth areas.

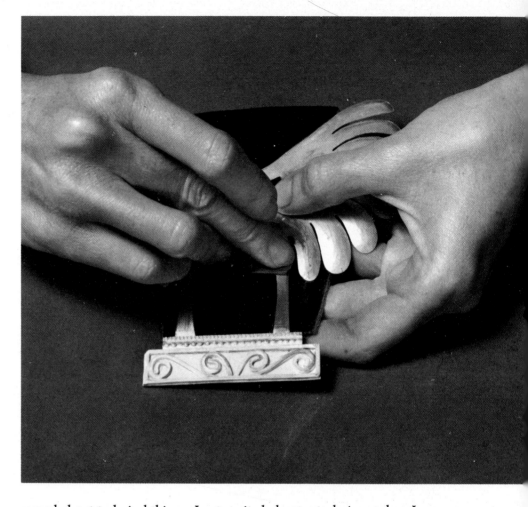

cerned about technical things. I get excited about a technique when I see someone else doing it or when I discover a different way of accomplishing something, but my designs are never based on technique. They are all based on ideas, and I use whatever technique is suitable to accomplish the idea. I have to admit that designs can be limited by one's technical vocabulary, so I'm never unwilling to learn new techniques when the need arises. However, I do consider technique a handmaiden to the idea and the form, which are all-important in the making of any work of art.

I like to work directly in the material. I avoid indirect processes, not so much because I get satisfaction out of the actual process, but because I feel I can control it better. I don't like things that get out of my hands, because then I'm not sure of what's going to happen. I prefer to

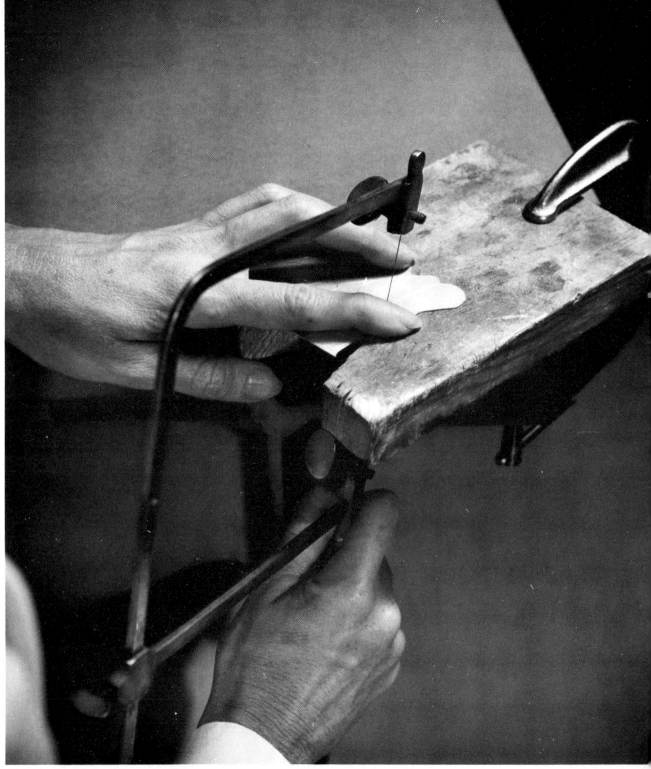

Figure 13. The chain units are sawed out of 24-gauge sterling sheet. There
will be twelve identical units and two end units, which will be fashioned into
hooks for attachment to the pendant.

Figure 14. The chain units are dapped into a hollow depression on a lead block in order to give a dome shape to the rounded end.

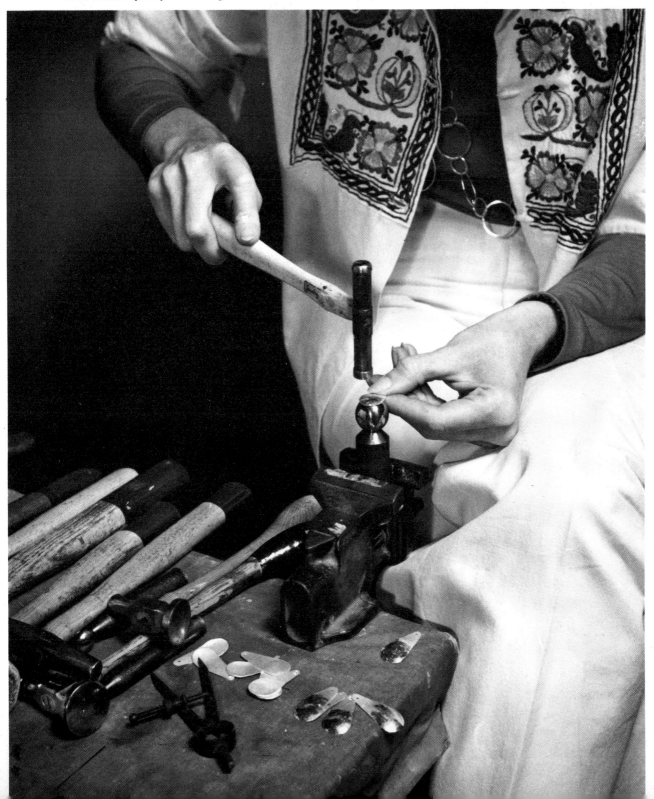

Figure 15. Each of the units is annealed and then planished over a dapping punch to refine the form and the surface. The chain elements will have the same textural quality as the wing feathers.

know what will happen. Some people just like working in a material, using their hands and their skills. I'm not one of them. In fact, there are times when I hate the whole process, and other times when I find the actual making of a piece rather tedious. I'm really interested only in the end product, and that makes me go where I go and do what I do. I have a compulsion to accomplish what I have in my head in the most exciting way possible. I am eager to get to the end, to see the results, and to enjoy the realization of my idea, and I am willing to spend any amount of time, effort, and energy that it takes to get to that point.

The piece I am making here is one of a series of torso pieces based on classical motifs. A fragment of a torso will be combined with wings and architectural elements to produce a pendant-brooch, a piece that can either be worn around the neck or pinned to a garment. The chain will be integrated into the piece by a repetition of the feather form, but it will be easily removable to allow the pendant to be worn as a brooch. The torso series (of which this is the third) combines various classical themes: the wings of a sphinx; a softly modeled nude; and an architectural form of pedestal and columns. This particular piece will use *millefiore* glass (which is also classical in origin) made by Richard Ritter, a resident glassblower at Penland.

I start with a freehand sketch, which establishes the mood and character of the piece as well as its general form. This is not a working drawing but rather a reminder of the spirit and feeling of the piece. I will make some paper patterns to determine size and proportion, and one of these will be glued to a sheet of metal as a template when I begin to work. I keep the sketch at hand as I am working and let it dictate the kinds of details and embellishments that are added to the piece as it develops. I find this is essential if the piece is to be finished with the same spirit and life it had when it was first conceived on paper.

The piece will be approximately 6 inches by 6 inches, with the torso about 3 inches by 1½ inches. Part of the torso will be covered by the column structure and will be reinforced on the back by additional columns of sheet metal. The torso will be attached to the piece with rivets rather than with heat, since the metal is very thin and needs both protection and a minimum of heating.

The torso is made simply by embossing a very thin sheet of fine silver with a burnisher, pushing the metal into a soft pad of leather and newspaper. (Figure 1) It is worked from both sides, back and front. The technique is very close to repoussé, except that tools and a hammer are

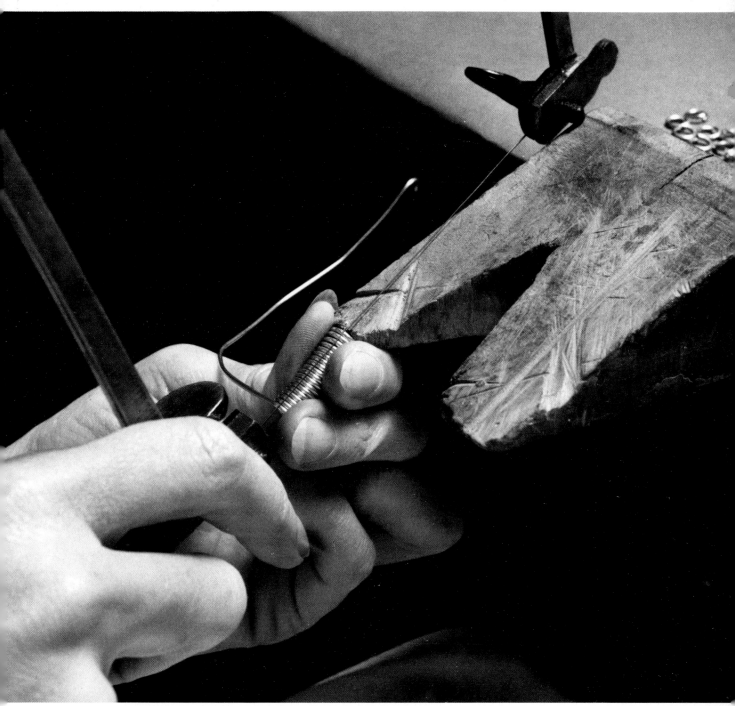

Figure 16. Jump rings for joining the chain units are made by coiling wire around a large nail. A single saw cut divides the coil into multiple rings of the same dimension.

Figure 17. A jump ring is inserted into a hole drilled in the small end of each chain unit. It is closed and filed flat across the joint in preparation for soldering. The chain is assembled by soldering the ring of one unit to the recessed area of the next unit.

not used, because the metal is thin and soft enough to be manipulated and modeled by hand. This technique was used extensively in classical times with gold, to make both funerary masks and multiple elements that were sewn to garments. The metal was simply pushed into a press mold (probably made of carved wood) with a tool similar to the burnisher I use. I am very interested in this technique and its possibilities. At some time in the future I will pursue the idea of making a mold out of plaster, clay, or wood and use it to make multiple images. However, right now, since I am only making one, I will work directly, using a burnisher and a pad of paper. (Figure 2)

The whole pendant form of wings, columns, and pedestal is cut from a single sheet of 20-gauge sterling silver, using a jeweler's saw and one of the paper patterns. (Figure 3) The wings are to have some dimensional quality, which I will add directly with hammers rather than by chasing, since the forms are simple and large enough to be worked in this way. The feathers are first hit from the back with a hammer while resting on a grooved lead block, which functions as a die to control the depth and curvature of the form. (Figure 4) Working this way requires some care and precision in directing the hammer blows, but since it is so much quicker than chasing, I use it as much as possible. (Figure 5) After all the feathers on both wings have been dapped in this fashion, the surfaces are thoroughly scrubbed with steel wool to remove all traces of lead that may have been deposited, since heating will cause even the smallest particle of lead to eat a hole in the silver. The whole piece is then annealed and pickled. Several stakes or anvils are improvised from various hammer heads and several sizes of dapping punches, to enable me to work with a hammer on the front of the wings. By using a highly polished and very small flat hammer, I am able to planish each of the feathers by resting it on a suitably shaped steel form and hammering lightly over the whole surface. The planishing refines the form, providing that I rest the silver firmly against the steel stake and place the hammer blows at the point of contact. This requires moving each feather slowly back and forth across the stake as I hammer, since the form is longer than the stake but must have the same contour throughout its entire length. By hammering carefully, I am also able to produce an evenly faceted texture over the entire surface of each wing. The column and pedestal areas are not hammered at all, but are kept flat and smooth with light taps of a rawhide mallet.

The pedestal area needs to be ornamented in a way that will provide thickness and weight as well as decorative detail. A frame of 10-gauge square wire is soldered together and filled with several scrolls of

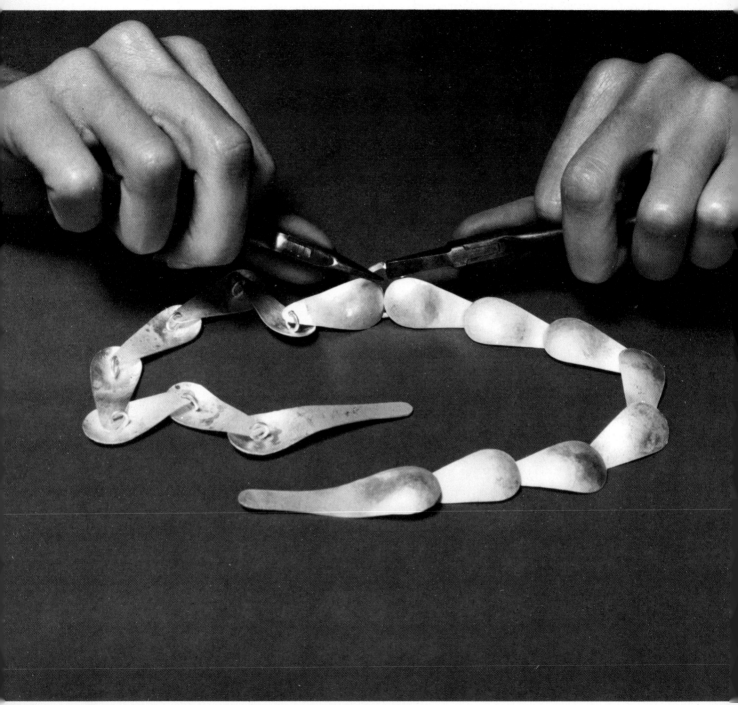

Figure 18. Since the chain has a directional design, it is made in two halves, with the rounded ends facing away from the pendant. The halves are joined at the back with a large ring of square wire, which allows the chain to move freely as it goes around the neck.

the same weight wire. The classical theme is repeated in the use of details resembling those carved on lintels and architraves of classical temples and sarcophagi. (Figure 6) The whole ornament is soldered together using hard solder, filed flat on the back, and soldered flush to the sheet-metal form with medium solder. (Figure 7) Between the soldering operations, the pieces are thoroughly cleaned in warm pickle to ensure a good fit and to aid in building up a deposit of fine silver on the surface, which will be used to achieve the final finish of the piece.

Since the torso will be positioned and fastened on the back of the piece, an aperture must be cut in the piece that will accurately conform to the outline of the relief. This is done first with a paper pattern, traced from the back of the torso, which is glued to the back of the main form. Holes are drilled in the four corners of the form, a saw inserted in one, and the section cut out accurately around the paper pattern. The edges of the opening are filed and minor corrections made where necessary to accommodate the torso perfectly. (Figure 8)

The two *millefiore* glass slabs I have decided to use as further ornamentation were graciously donated by Richard Ritter, who makes the most beautiful variations of this ancient technique. He has already cut the glass rod into thin slabs, which have a frosty appearance from the cutting process. I want them polished on one side and I do this in the lapidary shop, using a variety of fine and finer grits and a final buffing with a metal oxide. The glass will be set like stones, using a bezel mounting made of fine silver sheet strips shaped to each slab, soldered, reshaped, and soldered again to a base plate of 24-gauge sterling. (Figures 9, 10) I want the glass to be almost flush with the surface, so holes are cut in the wings to receive the two mountings. I have left a ledge of 1/16 inch all around the bezels, which provides a solid support for soldering the mountings into position. The ledge is ornamented on the back side with saw cuts and file marks all the way around to provide decorative detail and to soften the construction edges. When the mountings are completed, they are soldered into position from both the back and the front to ensure a complete joint.

The fittings for both the chain ends and the pin stem are soldered into place with easy solder. Simple oval jump rings will receive the hooks of the chain near the end of each top feather. The pin fixtures are positioned carefully to ensure that the pin stem will be totally invisible when not in use—a necessity since the piece will be used both as a pendant and as a brooch.

The whole piece is carefully gone over with abrasives of various

Figure 19. The chain receives the same finishing treatment as the pendant, except that fewer abrasives are used in order to preserve the hammered texture. The final polish is produced by thoroughly scrubbing the chain with a brass wire brush saturated in a solution of liquid detergent and water.

kinds to remove scratches and blemishes. (Figure 11) I most often use hand techniques, with emery papers and Scotch stone, but I want a highly polished area around the stones and along the columns to contrast with a softer finish on the torso and wings. This is done with a bristle brush and tripoli on a motor-driven polishing wheel, followed by a light buffing with muslin wheels and white diamond. After a thorough washing, the piece is subjected to a series of heating, cooling, and pickling operations to restore the fine silver surface, which is then scrubbed vigorously with a brass wire brush saturated in liquid detergent. (Figure 12)

The torso will be held to the body of the piece with silver rivets fashioned from 18-gauge sterling silver wire. The wire is beaded on one end, inserted into the front of a draw plate, and hammered on the thickened end to form a neat and slightly faceted head. The torso is taped into position, and holes to receive the rivets are drilled simultaneously through both pieces. Two extra column forms of 22-gauge sheet are added on the back to reinforce that rather weak area, and these are also drilled to receive the same rivets. All three pieces are held in place by inserting the rivet from the front and setting it with light blows of a rivet hammer on the back.

The glass slabs are set in their mountings after the metal underneath has been burnished to a mirror finish. The bezel is worked over with a burnisher until it fits snugly and the glass is held firmly. A detail of small engraved lines radiating from the bezel is added at the very end to soften the junction between the metal and the glass.

The chain is made of small teardrop-shaped units, which are domed on a lead form and planished over a dapping punch to achieve the same shape and surface as the wing feathers. (Figures 13–15) The units are assembled with a single jump ring, which is placed in a hole at the small end of each unit, closed, and soldered to the recessed area of the next unit. (Figures 16, 17) Since the chain is directional in design, it is made in two halves, with the rounded ends facing upward from the pendant. The two pieces are joined at the back with a large ring of square wire, which allows the chain to move freely as it is slipped over the head. The units at each end are then fashioned into simple hooks, which fit the oval jump rings very snugly and hold the chain firmly to the pendant. (Figure 18) The chain receives the same finishing treatment as the pendant, except that fewer abrasives are used in order to preserve the hammered texture. The same final polish is given the chain, with a thorough scrubbing by a brass wire brush saturated in a solution of liquid detergent and water. (Figure 19)

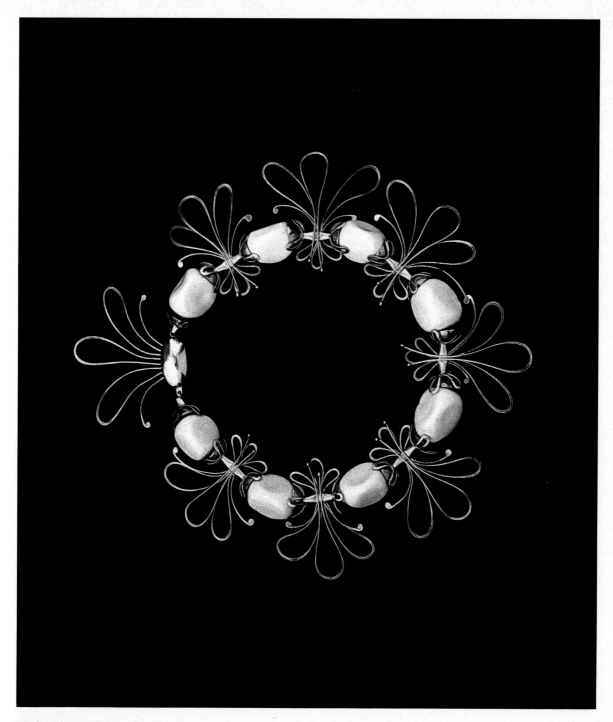

Beads. Silver and thrown porcelain

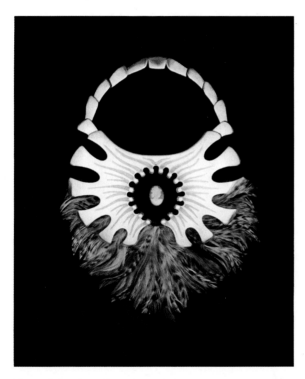

Pectoral. Sterling silver, fire-gilt, leather, feathers, cameo, pearls; 10″ high x 7″ wide

Pendant-brooch, "Torso II." Sterling silver, fire-gilt, ivory inlay

Brooch, "My Friend Curly." Sterling silver, fire-gilt, tourmaline crystals; 2″ high x 3″ wide

111

Plexiglas Pin
Bob Ebendorf

Bob Ebendorf, in his work, marries many different kinds of materials. Recently he has been creating pieces of jewelry from Plexiglas, combining this relatively new material with gold, silver, and pearls.

Bob Ebendorf was born in Topeka, Kansas. He received both the B.F.A. and M.F.A. degrees from the University of Kansas, and further studied at the University of Oslo and the State School for Applied Arts and Crafts in Norway.

His work has been exhibited nationally and internationally in numerous shows, including the Museum of Contemporary Crafts in New York; International Light Industries and Handicrafts in Munich, 1970; Goldsmith '70 and Goldsmith '74 Exhibitions; Viners of Sheffield, England; the Everhart Museum and Craft Alliance in Saint Louis, Missouri; and a solo exhibition at the Fairtree Gallery in New York, 1974.

His work is in the collections of Leonard Baskin; R. Phillip Hanes; Clemson University in Clemson, South Carolina; Illinois State University in Normal; the Museum of Art in Charlotte, North Carolina; the Saint Paul Museum of Art in Saint Paul, Minnesota; the University of Georgia in Athens; the University of Western Illinois in Macomb; the Medical College of Georgia in Augusta; Indiana State University in Terre Haute; and the North Carolina Council on the Arts.

He is president of the Society of North American Goldsmiths.

Bob Ebendorf has taught at Arrowmont Craft Workshop in Gatlinburg, Tennessee; Haystack Mountain School of Crafts, Deer Isle, Maine; State University College in New Paltz, New York; and Penland School of Crafts. He lives in Highland, New York.

Plexiglas Pin. Plexiglas, silver, pearls; 3½″ high x 3½″ wide·

My introduction to jewelry making was in high school, as a member of that general crafts class that always seems to be filled with "hard-to-teach" students. I made the typical copper pin and other small copper forms. I had a teacher who encouraged me. She saw that I had an interest in metalwork and she wanted to develop that interest.

During my senior year in high school I participated in a field trip to the University of Kansas, which is not far from my home town of Topeka. I spent the afternoon in the university art department, watching students at work. After that visit I was more than just interested in jewelry. I went on to earn a B.F.A. degree from the university in the area of gold- and silversmithing.

In graduate school I studied three-dimensional design as it related to crafts, and took as many gold- and silversmithing courses as I could. Though the university design department gave me a good understanding of basic design and drawing, I realized I needed more experience in dealing directly with metals. After completing my M.F.A., I was fortunate enough to receive a Fulbright grant, which enabled me to study in Norway for a year at the State School for Applied Arts and Crafts.

In Norway I learned many new ways of working with metals and new materials. I also learned how to handle tools and how to take care of them, and a great deal about the importance of precision in gold- and silversmithing.

Sometime later I was awarded a Louis Comfort Tiffany grant, and I returned to Norway. This time I worked in a small production studio and was exposed to the kind of thinking, work habits, and basic methods that are part of such an operation. For one year all I did was file and solder, file and solder. This experience taught me a lot about how to make a living from my craft, if I ever might want to live entirely from my work.

I learned, too, about making mass-produced jewelry. In a university atmosphere a student can design and make the kind of forms he wants, without caring about whether they will sell. He makes a form because he believes in it. But there is a different audience outside the university, with different demands. A craftsman must realize who this audience is and how to deal with it.

I've learned much about form, metal, and the uses of materials by going to museums; they have been like research centers for me. I can see the heritage the goldsmiths and silversmiths have handed down, and I feel I'm part of it. It surprises me that today I'm using many of the same tools and some of the same techniques that were used in the Middle Ages. Going to museums has thus helped me better understand what early

Figure 1. The pieces are cut from a flat piece of 20-gauge silver.

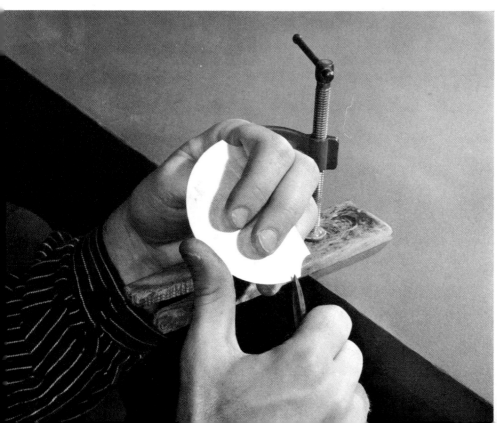

Figure 2. After sawing, the edges are cleaned with a scraper.

Figure 3. To drill the holes, the metal is placed on a board flush against a nail to hold it in place.

craftsmen did, and I've learned how to use their techniques in my work.

When I first started working in metals all I thought of was soldering. I thought of it as the only way to hold things together permanently. I had learned in Norway how to solder well, and how to construct. But sometimes one doesn't have the money to go out and buy all the necessary equipment, so I began to think of a new way of working—using cold connections, which means putting pieces together not with solder, but with rivets, nuts and bolts, and sleeve fittings, or even by folding a piece of metal against itself. For instance, tinsmiths and people who do metalwork for heating and air-conditioning companies take large sheets of thin metal; by putting a crease here and a bend there they can establish a strong structural piece of metal.

I find that now I'm using a combination of solder techniques and cold connections, and this has opened up new possibilities in constructing pieces. Delicate work can be done where soldering isn't possible, by putting pieces together with sleeve fittings or carefully working with rivets. This method offers the added advantage of working with materials that will not tolerate heat.

At one time I worked only in silver. Now I've gotten away from a purist attitude. If I think a piece of Plexiglas will work in the design of a piece, I'll use it. I don't think it's an injustice to combine different materials. The piece I'm working on here is constructed of 20-gauge sterling silver and a combination of Plexiglas and pearls.

For the past few years my work has dealt primarily with surface enrichment. It's a very direct kind of involvement with the metal—in manipulation of the materials. And it doesn't require a lot of equipment. I can relate this to African cultures and the direct metal they use in their jewelry. The Africans use hammers and simple hand tools without power equipment. I do engraving, score into the metal, use chasing tools for embellishing the metal, use the saw blade graphically to cut into the metal and obtain negative and positive space relationships. Often I take a sharp scribe and just draw directly on the surface. For me, this directness is rich!

I find that I don't use buffers and polishing machines much any more. I seldom put a high finish on a work. The polishing I'm doing now is by hand: scraping and burnishing. I think that many people go through

Figure 5. Surface details are added with a stamping tool while the metal is still flat.

Figure 4. The metal is scored before being bent to a right angle.

Figure 6. Cross-hatch lines
define the pyramids.

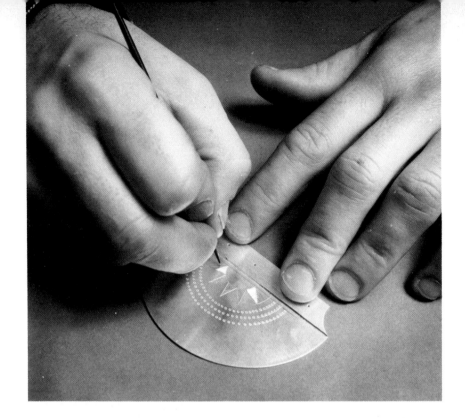

changes in individual technical processes. I certainly have! I have gone
from high polishes to matte finishes to sandblast finishes. Hopefully, I
am always open to new directions and continually moving into areas that
are new for me. It's like having a personal dictionary. I gain a technique,
or a word, or the understanding of a tool and become proficient with it;
then I record it, and when I'm making either conversation or jewelry, I
can just reach in and pull the "word" out and use it.

The pin I'm making is first conceived with a series of drawings.
The drawings, however, are loose, so that I can interpret and work from
them, making decisions and changes if needed as I go along. Sometimes
jewelers draw the design on paper, glue it to the metal, and cut out the
form, but I like working the drawings directly onto the metal.

I begin by cutting the form from a flat sheet of 20-gauge silver,
after having first drawn the shape on the metal. (Figure 1) Because of the
size of the piece, it's not necessary to use the clamp; I just hold the metal
with my hands. I use a jeweler's saw to cut it. This is a personal prefer-
ence. I could easily cut it out with table or bench shears, but in using them
I find I do not always get the form I want. I would rather take the time
and use a jeweler's saw; that way I know I'll have the two forms alike.

I cut the piece out, work the edge with a scraper, and then I'm ready to go on to the next piece.

For fast cutting or for cutting thick metal, I use a coarse blade, a No. 2 or 3. If I want to cut a delicate design, one that might be in close quarters, I'll go to a finer blade. After I cut the piece out, I file it down. I want it correct because I'm going to use it as a model for my second cut form. I also clean the edges. (Figure 2) This is a particular idiosyncrasy of mine; I like to have the metal feel pleasant in my hands. I file the edge, then use the scraper, then work the edge with an emery cloth.

Many beginning jewelers aren't really aware of what they are doing when they are filing. They do not watch to see how the file meets and relates to the metal. I can see by the brightness of the metal what areas are being filed away quicker than others. I work then for uniformity. Some beginners also lose the corner of a piece by filing *over* the corner.

I then steel-wool the two pieces—clean them off—and tape them together in order to cut five holes in the base of the piece. (Rubber cement can also be used to hold the pieces together.) The holes will not only be used for decorative purposes, but will be the main points for holding the three elements together. It is important to drill the holes precisely. At first I drill them quite small; eventually I will enlarge them. It is easier,

Figure 7. The metal is pressed into a right angle with the strength of the fingers.

Figure 8. A piece of solder is placed at the top of the seam. When it melts, the strip of solder is applied.

b

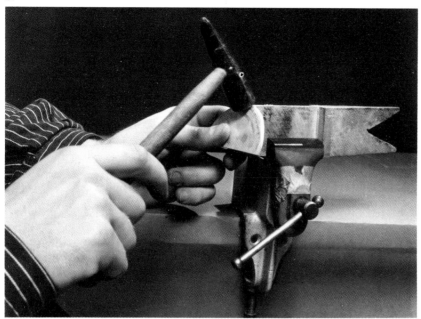

Figure 9. The edge of the flat decorative area is turned up in stages, against different surfaces.

c

I've found, to run the holes small, and then step up the bit size once I am further along on the construction of the piece.

When working alone, I've found it easiest to drill a piece of metal by hammering a nail into a board and placing the metal flush against it. (Figure 3) This keeps the piece from turning when I drill.

I drill the two plates while they are in flat sheet forms, but in my design I want right angles. Right angles are achieved by scoring the plates, then bending the metal to the correct angle. Scoring tools can be made from old files or purchased from tool and supply outlets. The scoring tool, which makes a V in the metal, is like a pocketknife; each cut pulls away a small bit of metal. (Figure 4) I continually check the back of the plate until I see a small, subtle line appear. Then I know the cut is deep enough for the metal to be bent.

Scoring is a technique many people forget to use. One way to become familiar with it is to get thick drawing paper and an Exacto knife, and practice forming with this tool. When actually working, it is important to remember that the impression should not be made too deep or the piece will break in two. When approaching scoring in metal for the first time, take copper or brass and do a sample model, then go on to more expensive materials.

Many beginners don't want to take that extra step; they want to hurry ahead on the project. When I work I'm not in that great a hurry. I work slowly and try not to make mistakes. I'd rather spend forty-five minutes setting or fitting up a piece properly than do it in a rush and do it incorrectly. So, I always have a scrap of copper or brass around and work on it first to see how deep I should make the V-cut before starting on a piece.

By using the scoring method, I find that the work is faster and cleaner, and I have very little excess soldering to clean up. It is only another way of working, another attitude. I enjoy the visual experience of seeing the metal shape itself.

While the metal pieces are still flat I do the surface details. By using a stamping tool and merely pressing on it with the strength of my hand, I impregnate the surface enough so that an image is left on the metal. (Figure 5) If I were to go back and use emery paper, polishing wheels, and compounds I could polish away the subleties of the surface

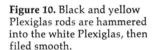

Figure 10. Black and yellow Plexiglas rods are hammered into the white Plexiglas, then filed smooth.

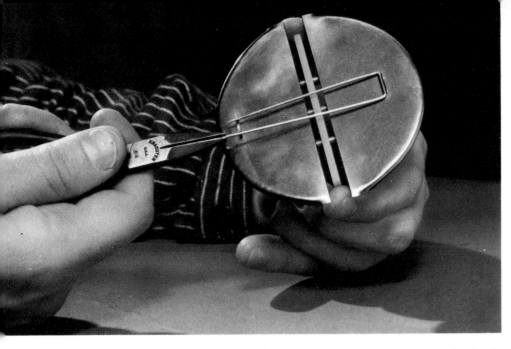

Figure 11. Nickel rod and a piece of tubing are used to make the back pin.

treatment, but this piece has already been properly brought to the finish I want. Once I have done the surface enrichments, I won't do any more polishing; all I'll need to do is clean up after a limited amount of soldering.

The tools I use for embellishing are nothing more than drill and stock, purchased at a hardware store and filed to a tapered point. I've drilled a slight indentation in the center of each of the drill rods, each drill being a different size. There are fifteen rods, and because I have graduated each of the holes, their impressions will vary. It is with these tools that I make the small round circle shapes on the metal surface. If I were to strike them with a hammer, the visual impression would deepen; but here I want only a subtle suggestion on the surface.

Look at Russian icons! Some of those beautiful surface impressions have been pressed through gold leaf. Basically I have done the same thing, pressed into the surface. As you look at an icon, you can see the surface impression. You can also find additional depth in the details. That's what I try to do: give my work a feeling of different levels of participation. I want activity on two and three and even four levels. It might be done with metals, surface decorations, changes of shape. I enjoy surprising the viewer's eye.

The embellishment technique might at first appear easy, but it's not. It takes time and patience, particularly to learn how to use and hold the tools. The design I have decided on for these two plates is developed first with quick sketches. It consists of a set of three dotted rainbow

Figure 12. A probe pin guides the chips of solder into place. If a probe pin is not available, a clothes hanger may be used.

Figure 13. Yellow Plexiglas rods are heated in water and bent into shape while they're hot.

arches, underneath which is a sunburst. The rays of the sunburst are a series of sharp pyramids, which I've drawn directly into the metal. (Figure 6) To establish the pyramids I have worked cross-hatch lines in one set, then drawn another set of pyramids behind. Finally I put a series of dots inside the sunburst itself.

After finishing the surface decoration and scoring the piece, it is necessary to bend the plates. All you need is a sharp right angle to bend the metal over; the edge of a table will do. I use a surface plate and press the metal down and over the edge with my fingers. (Figure 7) If necessary, I could use a rawhide mallet to pound the metal, but if the piece has been scored properly it will bend over the edge like tissue. The bend will be clean and straight and will form a right angle. The piece is in a delicate state now and should not be mishandled by resetting the angle; otherwise the metal will break. Later, I will flow solder in the weak area to strengthen it.

Another thing that beginning metalsmiths often forget is that in soldering, the surface of the metal should be clean. The metal may look clean, but if it has been handled often, oil has been left on it, and this film prevents the solder from flowing correctly.

In preparation for soldering I make sure all my materials and tools are handy. This is very important to me. It might take an extra twenty minutes in the setup, but the time is well spent because less time will be needed later for cleaning up a piece that is improperly soldered.

I clean my solder stick with emery paper and then flux the solder

124

stick. Finally, I flux the piece itself, using a clean brush and painting the total area that will be heated. I make sure that the flux goes down into the crease that will be soldered.

Because of the size of the piece of metal, I will need a large tip on the torch—a No. 4. I don't want to cause hot spots by using too small a tip and having the heat concentrated on a small section. When the piece is being heated, I want to know exactly when to come in with the stick solder. To alert myself to this, I cut a small piece of solder, place it at the top of the seam, and watch to see when it starts to melt. When it does, I apply the strip of solder. (Figure 8) Solder always flows toward heat, so I move my torch down the crease and pull the solder through the joint.

By doing it this way, I have only one spot to clean—at the top of the crease. I clean that spot with a file. If I had used chips of solder I would have had to clean up white marks all along the joint. After soldering, I place the piece in a warm solution of Sparex and water, which will clean the flux from it.

The metal is now bent at a 45-degree angle; the bent edge forms a wall in relation to the flat decorative area. Next I want to turn up the edge of the decorative area. I use a bone hammer, which is soft, and hit the metal with strong, sturdy blows, resting it on a tree stump. (Figure 9a) The metal begins to conform; the edge turns up subtly. I don't do it all at once; I turn the edge in three different steps.

After turning up the lip, or edge, on the tree stump, I move it to another piece of hard wood, which happens to be the edge of a bench pin, and drive the metal over the edge, coating it—as if I were raising the metal on a metal stake with a metal hammer—until the desired shape is produced. (Figure 9b)

After hammering, I anneal the metal form to soften it for the next use of the hammer. The piece is quite hot after annealing, and I let it air-cool rather than quench it in water. If I were to put the metal directly into water it would warp or perhaps even crack. This is an important thing to remember, as a piece can be ruined this way: let the piece air-cool.

Turning the edge, the final step in hammering, is also done with the bone hammer. (Figure 9c) It is a slow and difficult step; I do not want to coax the metal too fast and create ripples. Though I still have a very subtle shape in the bend, it will be offset by the Plexiglas I am using in the center.

The Plexiglas is white opaque, and I will use an arch-shaped piece between the two silver shapes. I arrive at the shape I want by cutting out

Figure 14. The ends of the tubings are flared to hold the parts together.

125

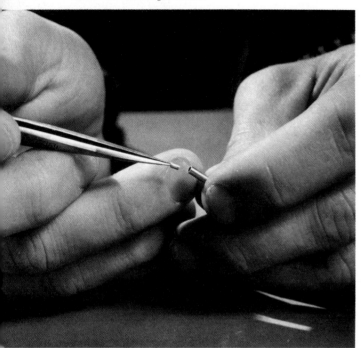

Figure 15. Small tubing is inserted in the larger tubes.

Figure 16. White pearls are glued to nickel wire at the ends of the tubes.

different paper forms from illustration board, a method that saves on materials. After deciding on the shape, I cut the piece. Plexiglas is an easy material to work with; it cuts and drills easily. In fact, it is no different to cut from silver or wood.

After cutting out the tonguelike form, I've found that the white has a raw appearance. To add some color to the surface, I take rods of yellow and black Plexiglas and cut small pegs from them. Next I drill two arch-shaped rows of holes in the white Plexiglas and drive the small pegs into the hole (Figure 10), then file them down level with the white surface. The white Plexiglas is now ready for final construction.

Returning to the sterling silver plates, I solder on the back pin. The back pin is easy to make: I simply cut a piece of silver tubing to the length I want and solder it to the back of the plate. Then I take a piece of nickel rod—because it has both strength and spring—and insert it into the tubing. I bend the nickel rod on both sides to a 45-degree angle. (Figure 11) This forms the pin that goes through the fabric. The latch for the pin is made by cutting out the block letter "C" from a piece of silver sheet. This is soldered on the back, directly under the tubing.

I also solder two pieces of tubing into the wall of each sterling

126

plate. In doing so, I prefer to push them through the metal instead of butt-joining them. This allows me to place chips of solder on the back side. Once they are in place—I use easy solder—I file off the excess on the back side. It is a quicker and cleaner method.

So that the holes will accept the four pieces of tubing (one piece at each end of each sterling wall), I enlarge the initial holes. As I said, I prefer to start with small holes and increase the bit size; I can then file the final size I want. It is a personal choice of method, and not necessary for every jeweler.

I have an iron probe pin handy to guide the chips of solder into place if they should move. (Figure 12) A clothes hanger can also be used for this purpose. After soldering, I place the piece in the pickle for cleaning.

The tubings are now set in place and ready for the next step, which is to add to them pieces of arched yellow Plexiglas. There are a number of ways that Plexiglas can be used. Flat sheets can be used decoratively by cutting and joining them with rivets, combinations of Plexiglas can be used, or Plexiglas can be formed or bent, which is what I plan to do with the yellow rods.

Plexiglas must be formed when it is hot. The piece is heated over a

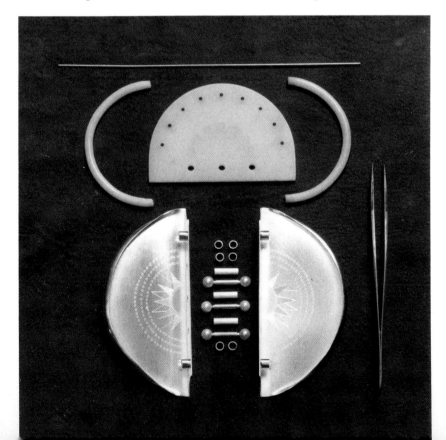

Figure 17. All the parts of the piece before assembly.

stove or in a pan of water, then formed, for example, over a broom handle, the piece being manipulated with just the pressure of the fingers. I find it works best to heat up a shallow pan of water and bring it to a boil before heating the rod. (Figure 13) When Plexiglas cools, it becomes hard; if the correct shape does not form immediately, drop the rod back into the water and reheat it.

When the Plexiglas rods have been formed and fitted into the silver tubes, I design and execute three center poles that will hold the entire piece—silver and Plexiglas—together. I cut three pieces of half-inch tubing and thin the walls with a file. At the same time I also cut six wafers from silver tubing one size larger than the three center poles. I fit the wafers between the white Plexiglas form and the top and bottom sterling plates, so that the Plexiglas appears to float in the middle. Then I take the three silver center poles and slip them through the corresponding holes in the Plexiglas form, the silver wafers, and the two silver plates. I flare the ends of the tubings with a dapping tool (Figure 14), which sets up a tension between the two pieces of silver and therefore holds the plates together.

Inside the three center tubes are fitted other, smaller tubes. (Figure 15) Then three pieces of nickel wire are cut to a length longer than the outside tube. A pearl with a small opening is fitted and epoxied to one end of each of the three wires (Figure 16), which are then threaded through the inside tubes in a snug fit, and a second pearl is epoxied on the other end.

When assembled the pin will contain the following elements (Figure 17): Two flat pieces of sterling that have surface embellishment, with the edges of the curved silver curled up and over, the end of each plate scored and turned up. In each of the plates there is a set of five holes, with pieces of tubing in the two end holes to hold an arched piece of yellow Plexiglas. The center holes are lined up in position to receive the three pieces of tubing that hold the plates together. Between the two plates of sterling silver is an upright piece of white Plexiglas, separated from the plates by two sets of silver wafers. The final elements are the three small tubes threaded with nickel wire, with pearls glued to each end.

Before I construct the piece, I heat up liver of sulfur and dip the two plates of sterling into the solution, being extremely careful not to touch the surface of the silver before it has been oxidized. (Touching the metal leaves fingerprint marks.) The liver of sulfur solution turns the silver a gunmetal gray. I then rinse off the piece and brass brush it to bring it to a soft gray look, and the piece is ready for assembling.

Pin. Ivory, pearls, Plexiglas, gold-plated bronze; 3½" high x 3½" wide

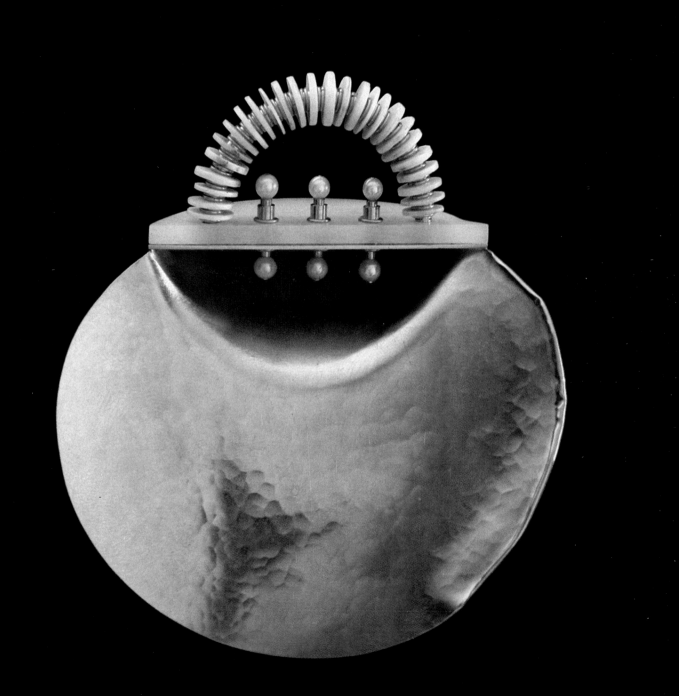

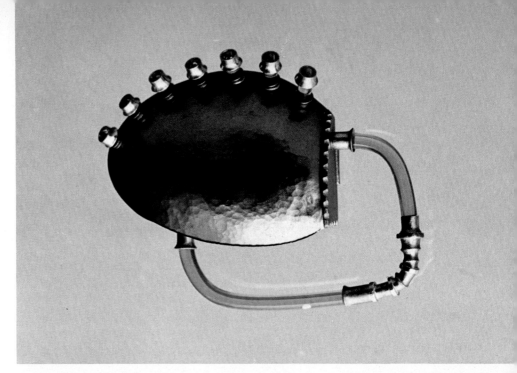

Pin
Plexiglas, pearls, silver;
3½" high x 3½" wide

Pin
Plexiglas, pearls, silver
gold-plated bronze;
4" high x 3" wide

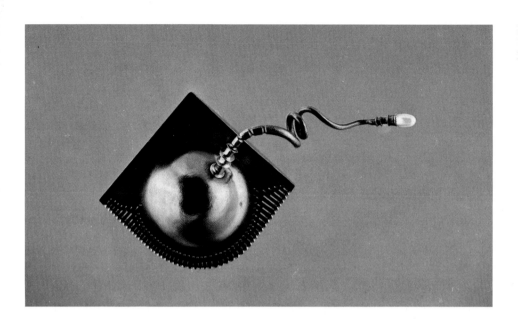

Pin
Silver, gold, Plexiglas,
pearl; 1½" high x 2¼" wide

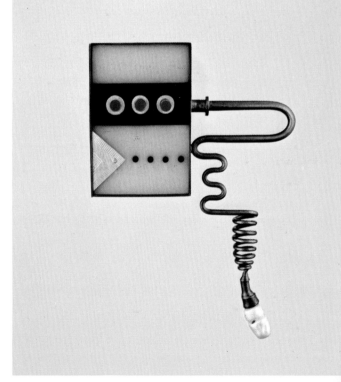

Pin
Silver, Plexiglas, pearls,
gold; 3" high x 1½" wide;
top 2"

Pin
Plexiglas, pearls, silver,
gold-plated bronze;
3½" high x 3" wide

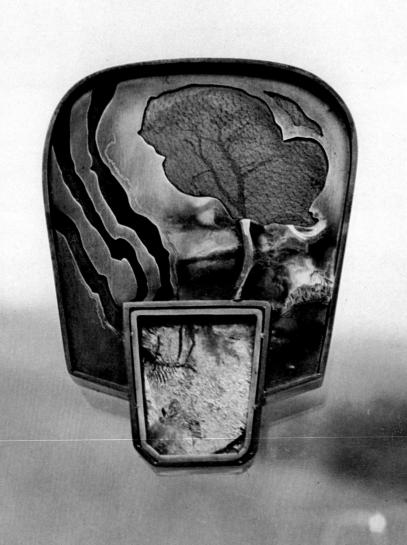

Mirror Image
Eleanor Moty

Eleanor Moty is best known for her work in photofabrication, a technical process that has opened up new possibilities in jewelry making. Her work is always well crafted and beautifully designed. It usually features some photochemical process, as well as many different and surprising types of materials.

Eleanor Moty was born in Chicago, Illinois. She received a B.F.A. from the University of Illinois, Urbana, and an M.F.A. from the Tyler School of Art, Temple University, Philadelphia.

Her work has been shown at the International Invitational Jewelry Exhibition in Munich, 1970 and 1972; Jewelry '71 in Toronto, 1971; Zlatarna Celje Invitational Jewelry Show in Yugoslavia, 1972; Eight American Metalsmiths in England, Photographic Directions at the State University of New York in New Paltz, and Goldsmith '74 at the Renwick Gallery of the Smithsonian Institution in Washington, D.C., 1974.

Her work is in the collections of the Minnesota Museum of Art in Saint Paul; Temple University in Philadelphia; J. Fred Woell, Cambridge, Wisconsin; Stanley Lechtzin, Philadelphia; and Georgia State University in Atlanta.

She is a member of the Society of North American Goldsmiths.

Eleanor Moty has taught at Arrowmont Craft Workshop, Gatlinburg, Tennessee; Moore College of Art, Philadelphia; the University of Wisconsin, Madison; Haystack Mountain School of Crafts, Deer Isle, Maine; and Penland School of Crafts. She lives in Madison, Wisconsin.

Mirror Image. Hand mirror made of fabricated silver, brass, copper, with photoprinted leather, amethyst, mirror; 2½" x 3¼" x ½"

I find it difficult to talk seriously about my work or to explain what it means beyond the technical aspect. I don't mean to be coy, but only close friends or those who care can realize the significance of various elements in each piece I make. Frankly, for me technique is secondary, even though I am probably best known for my use of a particular technical process, photofabrication.

I intend each piece to be a personal statement or time capsule of events in my life, experiences and things or people around me. I am not appealing to a mass audience. I produce only a few pieces a year, and I go to great lengths to find the materials or images I need to make an object exactly as I want it, even if this means reworking or remaking elements. My thought is that there should be more to each object than what is readily seen; the object should contain something personal. I don't want the work to enter the category of anonymous niceties; I am not making purely decorative jewelry.

I strongly avoid making jewelry or metal objects for myself. For me, the pleasure is in creating the work, not in wearing or owning it. I much prefer owning the work of my colleagues. Though I do make things to wear, I try not to be inhibited creatively by whether an object is wearable.

I often face problems in being categorized. People expect to see photofabrication in each object I make, but often I do not want to use this process in my work. Photofabrication is extremely time consuming; and, being people-oriented, I like to devote a great deal of my time to teaching, workshops, and lectures. Sometimes it is a relief to do straight fabrication without photo processes or electroplating. What this boils down to is my trying to do what I want to do when I want to do it and to be myself at the same time.

My first experience in jewelry came when I was a student at the University of Illinois in Champaign-Urbana. I was originally an art education major, but I quickly switched to jewelry after taking my first jewelry course in my sophomore year. I had the good fortune of working with Robert Von Neumann and later meeting J. Fred Woell. It was these two men who inspired and encouraged me. I like every aspect of dealing with metal: its working and esthetic properties, its mechanics and technology, and the fact that it allows so much room for exploration.

While I was an undergraduate I was introduced to two unique technical processes: electroforming and photofabrication. I had met an engineering student who knew about photofabrication in printed circuitry and who suggested we use it in jewelry. Soon after, while Robert

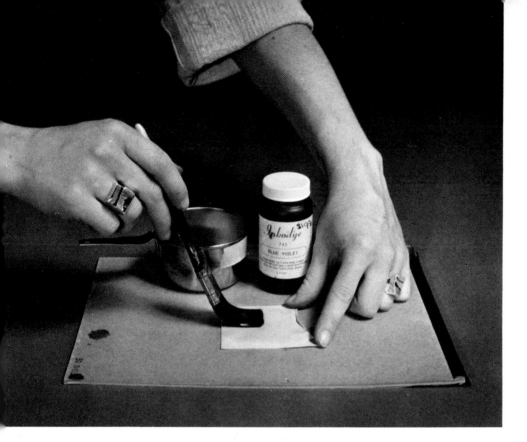

Figure 1. Inkodye—a photosensitive dye—is applied to the leather with a brush.

Figure 2. The negative is placed on the leather and dried under glass in the sun.

Von Neumann and I were researching electroforming in one of the Science Research Laboratories at the University of Illinois, I met the laboratory technician for photofabrication. I worked with this technician for two years and learned the process at an extremely high level of sophistication. It was these two processes, electroforming and photofabrication, that strengthened my involvement with jewelry. As a result I began searching for a graduate school.

I eventually selected Tyler School of Art at Temple University in Philadelphia for graduate work in metal. I was eager to study outside the Midwest, to develop a different outlook. Also, Stanley Lechtzin's involvement in electroforming at Tyler was an added incentive to my considering that school. Lechtzin's metal program was exactly what I wanted—very sophisticated and demanding—and Lechtzin was an excellent example and teacher.

Lechtzin encouraged me to continue my research in photofabrication. Since I no longer had access to the equipment I needed, I spent a great deal of time devising a less sophisticated setup for the process. I also began to use the image in a more dimensional way. I needed to work beyond flat images on flat pieces.

I received my M.F.A. from Tyler after three years, and it was

Figure 3. The design is traced with a scriber on the front and back of the metal.

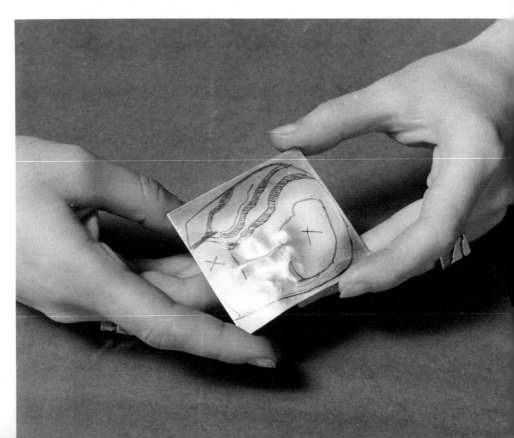

Figure 4. While working with the repoussé method, attention should be focused on the face of the tool and the metal. The tool is held off the surface of the metal.

Figure 5. The pitch is burned off the metal, which is then rinsed clean.

Figure 6. In chasing, the tool is kept on the surface of the metal, and overlapping blows are used.

Figure 7. The 16-gauge brass
sheet is folded into shape by
using a rawhide hammer.

Figure 8. Dividers are used
to scribe the line on the
bezel.

during my last year of graduate school that I began teaching jewelry and
metalsmithing at Moore College of Art in Philadelphia. I taught at Moore
for two years before going to the University of Wisconsin in Madison,
where I am now a visiting lecturer in jewelry and metalsmithing.

The mirror frame I'm making began with a stone hexagonal-
shaped crystal slab. I liked the shape and the color and natural imper-
fections within the stone. The frame will be totally fabricated with a
photo image of a tree that has some of the quality of the line in the
stone. Most of the design is directly related to the stone.

The first step is to photographically apply the tree image to
leather, an absorbent material. Under a safelite, I brush a photosensitive
dye—Inkodye—on the leather. (Figure 1) When the leather is nearly dry,
I place a negative of the tree on it and contact-print the leather under
glass in the sun. (Figure 2) Within minutes, the color comes up (in this
case, purple). When the color is intensified to the degree I want, I rinse
the leather, which stops the printing or development.

Part of the front of the frame is to be chased. In preparation for

Figure 9. A burin pulls up the burr in the brass to the line that has been scribed.

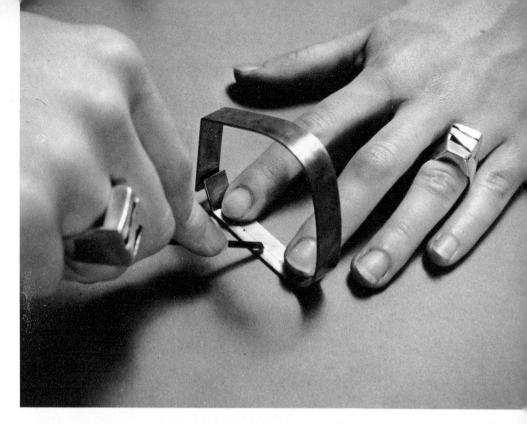

Figure 10. The bezel is fitted around the silver piece by hand.

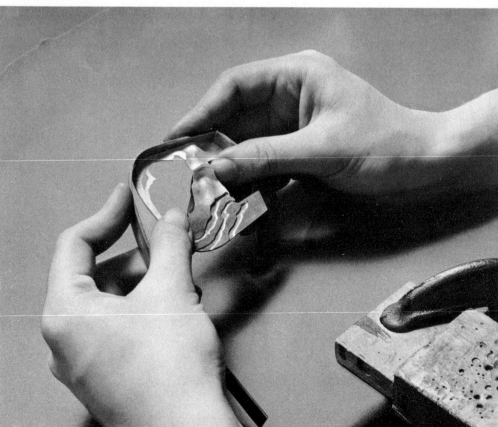

this I cut a sheet of 20-gauge silver oversize and, from an original sketch, trace the design on the front and back with a scriber. (Figure 3) I do not cut the silver to the exact size, because I will be placing it in pitch in order to do the chasing. The pitch will curl up over the edges of the metal to hold it, making it impossible to work on the actual edge.

I do the repoussé first. The pitch is heated with a torch, which softens it and allows it to receive the metal. Once the pitch hardens it holds the metal securely; at the same time it offers a resilient surface so that the metal can be worked down into it. The pitch bowl enables me to move the work around so that I have access to it from all sides.

Repoussé is the process of pressing the metal out from the back. The tools used for this process are rounded to avoid cutting or breaking through the metal. The silver is stretched in wide expanses to avoid thinning one area too much. As I work, I hold the tool slightly off the surface of the metal so that when I strike it with the chasing hammer, there's a jackhammer action. The chasing hammer has a very special

Figure 11. Kinks are put in the wire to allow for expansion when the metal is heated.

Figure 12. The bezel is filed
and fitted into place, then
soldered.

shape: the handle has a comfortable grip and a thin, springy midsection; the hammer head has a ball end and a broad striking face so that it is not necessary to watch the striking end of the tool. When working, I concentrate on the face of the tool and the surface of the metal, not the hammer. (Figure 4)

After shaping the metal from the back, I heat the pitch again, pull the silver out with tweezers, and burn the pitch that's stuck to the metal until it turns to ash. (Figure 5) I then rinse the metal until all the pitch is cleaned off. If the metal is not clean, the pitch will become embedded in the surface, which would create problems when I work on the front.

The metal is again set into the pitch, this time front side up. It is important to fill all the raised areas of the back with pitch so that they are all supported and firm.

Now I begin the detail work on the front, the chasing, using chasing tools. Some chasing tools have sharp edges for defining shapes, but I prefer working with rounded tools, to push parts of the metal together in order to create ridges and sharp forms. When chasing, I keep the tool on the surface of the silver and use overlapping blows to work the metal carefully and to define the shapes. (Figure 6) Here I have a

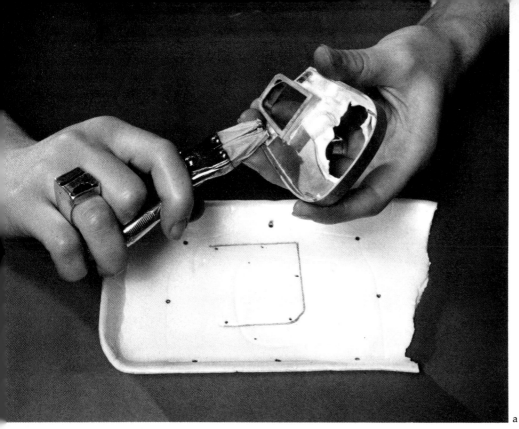

Figure 13. The correct holes in the silver back piece are established by using a thin sheet of styrofoam. An impression is made, lines drawn, and then the silver back piece is held in place while a marking pen sets the hole positions.

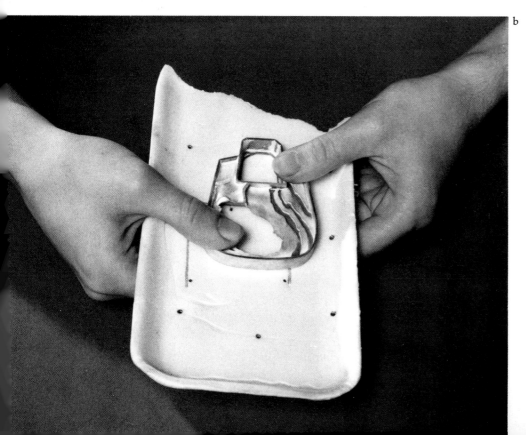

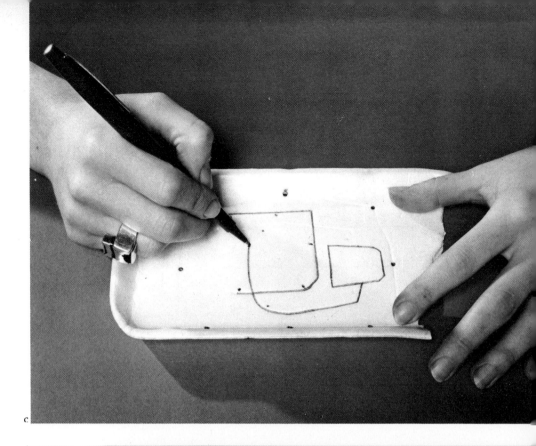

c

d

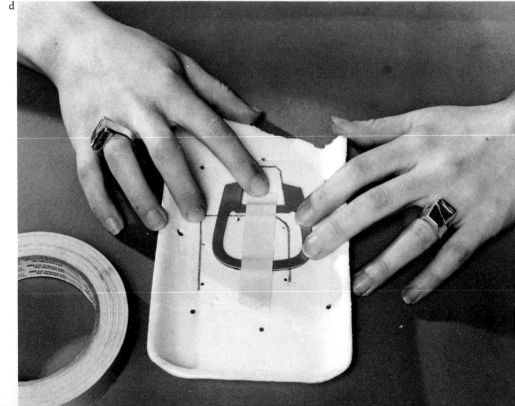

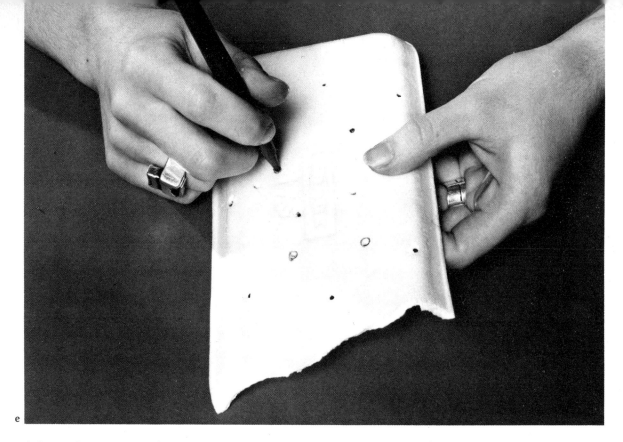

e

definite design in mind again—a continuation of the tree image I have applied to the leather.

After the chasing is finished I lay out the design very carefully in preparation for piercing the areas that will be backed with copper. I cut away the inside sections of silver and solder copper onto the cutaway area. Finally I cut away the section that will be filled in with the leather.

Next I score and fold a bezel of 16-gauge ¹/₄-inch brass sheet, which will fit around the silver at right angles. (Figure 7) Since the silver will be inset slightly below the top edge—floating—I make stitches to keep it positioned inside the brass bezel when it is soldered in place. I use dividers to scribe a line inside the bezel or where the silver will be placed. (Figure 8) Then, with a burin, or graver, I carefully pull up a burr in the brass, up to the line I have scribed. (Figure 9) The burrs, evenly spaced inside the bezel, keep the silver piece from dropping out of alignment when the bezel expands during soldering. The bezel is fitted around the piece by hand. (Figure 10)

In preparation for soldering the bezel around the silver, I bind the two pieces with iron binding wire to keep them positioned, looping the iron wire around the work and twisting the ends. If more tension is

Figure 14. The size of the rivets is checked with a drill gauge, and a large drill bit is used to countersink the holes.

needed I don't twist the ends tighter—the metal will expand as it is heated, and if the iron wire is too tight, it will dig into the softer metal. So I keep the wire slack, but put a kink into it in a couple of places with pliers; this way the iron wire can expand with the other metal. (Figure 11)

I make the bezel for the stone by scoring and folding 16-gauge 1/4-inch brass sheet. Next I cut away the section of the silver piece where the bezel for the stone is to be inset. (Figure 12) After filing and fitting, the bezel is soldered in place.

A pierced backing for the stone's bezel (20-gauge brass) is now soldered on from the back. I also make the 16-gauge square silver wire inset for the stone's bezel. This will be placed over the stone and secured with stitches to actually set the stone.

I trim and clean the edges of the brass-outlined frame with files and emery sticks and scribe the outside shape onto another silver piece that will be used on the back or glass mirror side. This backing is then pierced and filed.

Ordinarily, when I am making a mirror, I devise some way of taking the piece apart, in case the mirror breaks and needs to be replaced, but in this piece, to simplify things, I will just rivet the backing into place.

The rivets will go on the inside of the silver face section. In

Figure 15. The stone is set with a silver wire overlay.

147

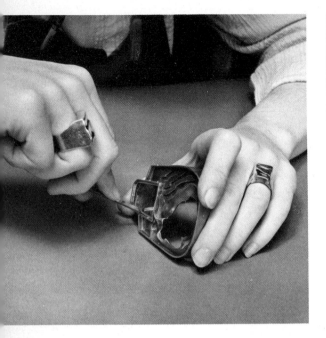

Figure 16. Stitches are used to hold the overlay in place.

Figure 17. *(above right)* Rivets are mushroomed with a riveting hammer.

preparation, I file or scrape the surface of the silver where they will be soldered. This is done to avoid soldering onto fire scale, which makes a weak joint. Then four 16-gauge silver wire rivets are soldered in place.

Corresponding holes must be drilled in the silver back piece. To determine the correct placement, I press the section with the rivets into a thin sheet of styrofoam, which makes an impression that I can trace with a marking pen. (Figures 13a–13c) I tape the silver back piece in place on the styrofoam impression and ink the silver with a marking pen through the holes made by the rivets. (Figures 13d, 13e) These pen marks allow me to drill accurately to the exact size of the rivet. I then use a large drill bit to countersink the holes. (Figures 14a, 14b) Finally, I finish and true up the surfaces of the metal with Nos. 320 and 600 emery paper, oxidize it with liver of sulfur, and use a soft wire brush to bring up a luster and burnish the metal surface.

Now the stone is set in the bezel with the silver wire overlay (Figure 15) and stitches (Figure 16), the leather is put in place with Dacron fluff as packing, the glass mirror is positioned, and the silver back piece is then riveted in place. The rivets are trimmed to a height of about half the thickness of the wire and are carefully widened with a riveting hammer or the ball end of a chasing hammer. (Figure 17) With that, the piece is completed.

Landscape. Handbag made of silver with silver photoelectroplated image, brass, assorted metal inlay, agate; 5¼" x 4" x 2"

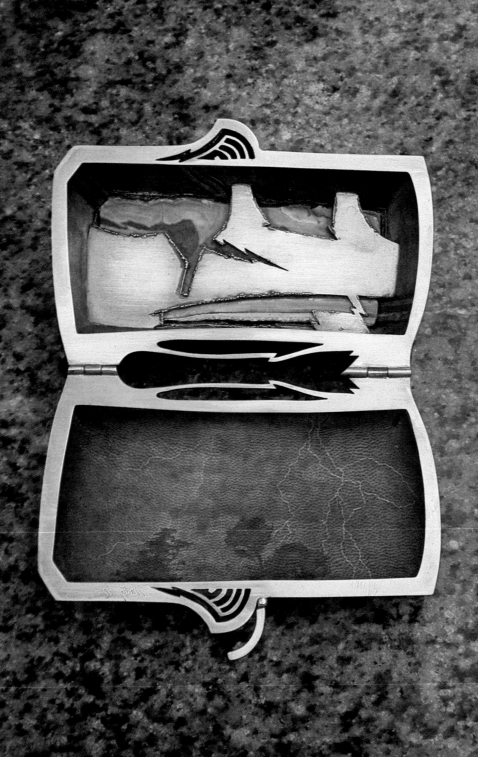

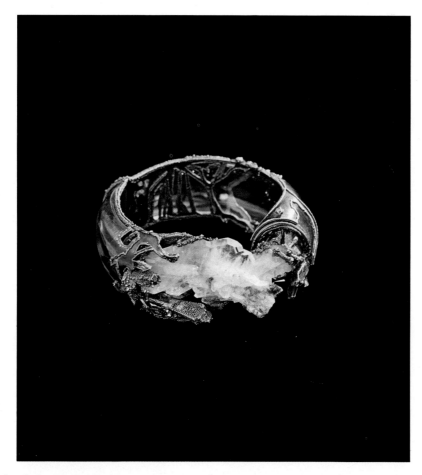

Choker Neckpiece. Photoetched
silver with silver electroplating
and electroforming,
Plexiglas, quartz
crystals; 7″ x 7″ x 2″

Lightning Box (interior). Silver with silver electroplate, brass, assorted
metal inlay, agate, photoprinted leather lining; 5¼″ x 3½″ x 2″ (closed size)

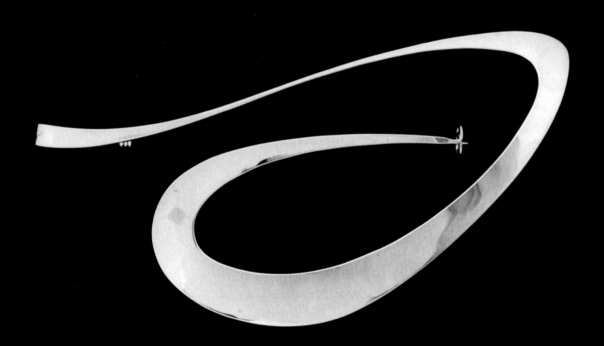

Silver Forged Pin
Ronald Hayes Pearson

Ronald Hayes Pearson has been a production metalsmith since 1948 and has worked successfully in all forms of metalsmithing. Throughout his career he has been particularly interested in forging various kinds of metal, from gold to iron. In this chapter he forges, from one piece of silver stock, a simple but elegant brooch.

Ronald Hayes Pearson was born in New York City. He attended the University of Wisconsin in Madison, the School for American Craftsmen at Alfred University, Alfred, New York, and the special design program of the Reed and Barton Silver Company.

His work has received numerous prizes and awards. It has been shown at many solo and group exhibitions in the United States and abroad, including the International "Good Design" Exhibitions at the Museum of Modern Art in New York, 1950–1954; annually at the Finger Lakes Exhibitions in Rochester, New York, 1950–1966; the Fiber–Metal–Clay Exhibit in Saint Paul, Minnesota, 1959 (where he took the first prize in jewelry); the National Religious Arts Exhibit (First Prize: Metal) in Birmingham, Michigan, 1960; the National Gold Medal Exhibit of the Building Arts, 1962; the Museum of Contemporary Crafts' Little Gallery (solo exhibition) in New York, and Eight by Eight at the University of Fine Arts in Dallas, Texas, 1963; Craftsmanship Defined at the Philadelphia Museum College of Art, 1964; the Invitational International Jewellery Arts Exhibition in Tokyo, The Iron Show in Rochester, New York, and Goldsmith '70 at Minnesota Museum of Art in Saint Paul, 1970; and the Memorial Art Gallery (solo exhibition) in Rochester, New York, 1971.

His work is in the collections of the Museum of Contemporary Crafts in New York; Sheridan College in Port Credit, Ontario, Canada; The Saint Paul Gallery and School of Art in Minnesota; the Memorial Art Gallery in Rochester, New York; The Johnson's Wax Collection; and many church and private collections.

He is a member of the Society of North American Goldsmiths.

Ronald Hayes Pearson has taught at the School for American Craftsmen, Alfred University; Berea College, Berea, Kentucky; Haystack Mountain School of Crafts, Deer Isle, Maine; and the Penland School of Crafts. He lives in Deer Isle, Maine.

Silver Forged Pin. One-piece forged sterling silver

I have been working in and making a living from metal since 1948. I was fortunate to have grown up in a rather special home environment. My father, Ralph M. Pearson, was an artist, teacher, and writer who had his own school in New York City and, during the summers, in Gloucester, Massachusetts, on an old 100-foot granite schooner. One summer, when I was about fourteen, a young metalsmith set up his shop in the hold of our ship, and I worked with him. This early experience, coupled with my admiration for and appreciation of the independent life my parents lived, definitely influenced my choice of career and life-style.

After five years in the Merchant Marine during World War II, I entered the School for American Craftsmen, which was then at Alfred University, and set up my first shop in an old chicken coop. At the end of that school year, with fifty dollars in hand, I struck out on my own. My original plan was to make sterling holloware. However, my first selling trip to New York City was a disaster, for there was no market for hand-raised silver made by a novice. And even if there had been, the dollar return would have been minimal. My dream of independence was in jeopardy: action was needed!

On the long, sad drive home, I tried to deal with realities. I did not have any jewelry-making experience—the school did not at that time include jewelry in its curriculum. Although it seemed the best course to follow, I had no time for exploration. Another answer had to be found, and it seemed to me that it had to involve a product that could be made quickly, in quantity, at a low price; that would appeal to the public; and that could be marketed in department stores as well as through the "contemporary" shops that were just beginning to come into existence. I decided that metal spinning was the answer. With borrowed money, I bought an old lathe, the tools of a retired metal spinner, wood for chucks, and several hundred pounds of commercial sheet bronze.

In the next seven years I worked harder physically than I ever had before or since—often as much as eighteen hours a day. I developed a group of about twenty designs: spun bowls, ashtrays, candle holders, desk accessories, and so on, ranging in diameter from three to fourteen inches. The work schedule went about as follows: one day cutting disks from rolls of 16-, 18-, and 20-gauge bronze with hand shears; one day spinning; one day trimming and making bases; and three days buffing. The pieces sold for $1.00 to $11.25 wholesale, and with an agent to handle distribution, I shipped all over the country. It was a very good experience, but I was delighted when a small specialty company asked for the rights

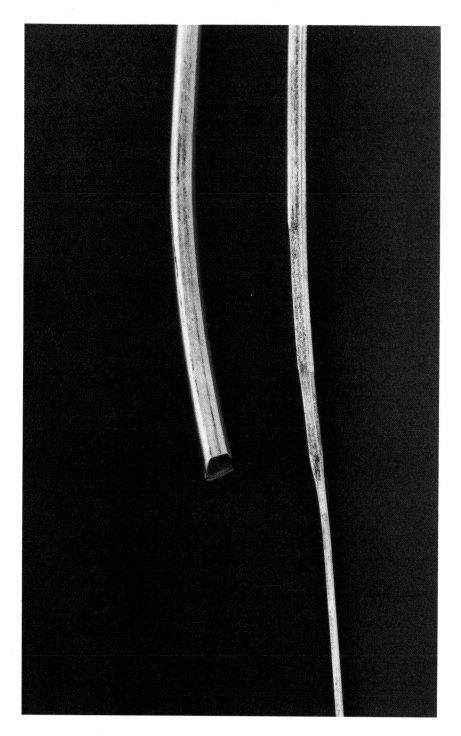

Figure 1. The pin is made from a single piece of 6-gauge square sterling wire, 9¾″ long (on left); it is rolled out to an eventual length of approximately 20″ overall.

Figure 2. Square rolling
redistributes material so that
the original design can be
achieved easily through
forging.

a

b

to produce some of the pieces. Several of the early bowls were selected for five successive "Good Design" exhibits at the Museum of Modern Art.

While involved with the spun bronze, I began to do jewelry, learning and exploring as I went along. In addition to production work, I have executed a vast number of commissions, both large and small, for private individuals, collections, churches, businesses, and universities. I have also served as a consultant for various industries and educational institutions.

Forging metal has always held a special fascination for me, and I've used the technique extensively. As my work increased in size, I began to think in terms of iron. In 1966 I built my first iron shop, and recently,

157

Figure 3. The shoulders left from rolling are removed by hammering, and the piece is straightened.

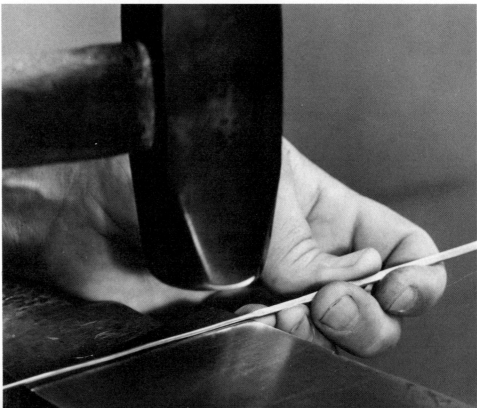

Figure 4. The pin stem is rounded.

Figure 5. The center curve of the piece is shaped over a depression in a wood stump.

following a move to Deer Isle, Maine, I built another. I expect to become increasingly involved in blacksmithing.

In 1952 I moved from Alfred to Rochester, New York, and with three partners opened Shop One, a retail craft shop that has functioned well through the years while maintaining high standards for the work that is shown.

When I started working in 1948, I had, as I still have, a strong desire to produce well-made multiples at reasonable prices so that many people could enjoy my products. I have consciously avoided cultivation of a "precious" feeling about my work. A successful piece of jewelry is one that complements and enhances the human form and personality. A

Figure 6. The center is spread on the anvil.

Figure 7. The left curve is shaped.

Figure 7. The left curve is shaped.

Figure 8. The left curve is planished on the anvil.

piece can be extremely simple or rather complex, as long as the human body does not become merely its pedestal.

How do I design a piece? I think, by dealing, probably unconsciously, with certain basics: a few tools, certain forms of materials, a few fundamental techniques, a client (who could be myself); and by drawing and building on the sum of my experiences. It's not particularly easy, but neither is it so very complicated. It just happens—as other things happen to other people. Most important, I like doing it. The piece I'm making is somewhat like a brushstroke (except that my brush is a hammer): it begins and it ends, and in between, there are a few gentle flourishes.

Forging is a method of redistributing metal from a stock form to a shape of the maker's choice. In essence, the basic principle is that when the cross peen strikes, it pushes the metal at right angles to itself; while a blow with the planishing face of the hammer spreads the metal evenly.

The forged pin I am making here starts with a $9^3/4$-inch piece of 6-gauge square sterling wire. (Figure 1) The widest point of the pin can be considered the center of the piece; this center is $2^3/4$ inches from the catch end and 7 inches from the pin stem point. The material is first distributed by tapering the wire with the square rolls of a rolling mill, as follows (Figure 2): on the short side, the first roll is made up to $1/2$ inch from the center; the second roll, to $1^3/4$ inches from the center; then six successive rolls are made, moving farther from center each time, till the silver is taken down to 11 gauge. The remainder is rolled out to 17 gauge and cut to a length of $1^1/2$ inches, to be used for the catch. For the long side, the first roll is made to within $1/2$ inch of center; the second roll, to within $4^1/2$ inches of center; the third, to $7^3/4$ inches of center; then $3/4$

Figure 9. The spiral catch is formed.

a

b

inch is left for each of the next two rolls, and the remainder is rolled down to 17 gauge, of which 6 inches is used for the pin stem.

A word here about the tools I use:

The rolling mill is a wonderful, time-saving piece of equipment that will do much more than simply decrease the gauge of a piece of stock. Tapering on the mill saves a great deal of time and makes it possible to use a minimal amount of material. The mill I use has two sets of 5-inch-wide rolls, one for flat stock and one for square stock, with nineteen steps.

The best anvil will have a hard flat surface free of indentations and scratches. It should be emeried with fine paper before work is begun, and kept clean and free from dirt and grit while working. For hammering, I use a 32-ounce cross peen sledge with both the planishing face and the

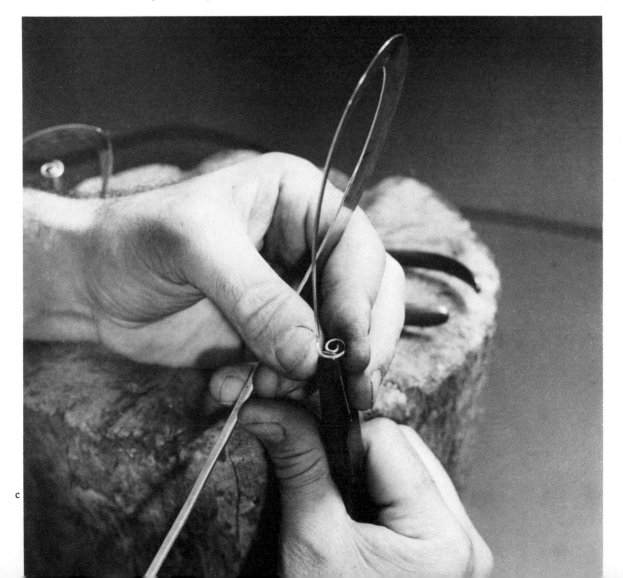

c

Figure 10. The vertical plane
on the right end is forged.

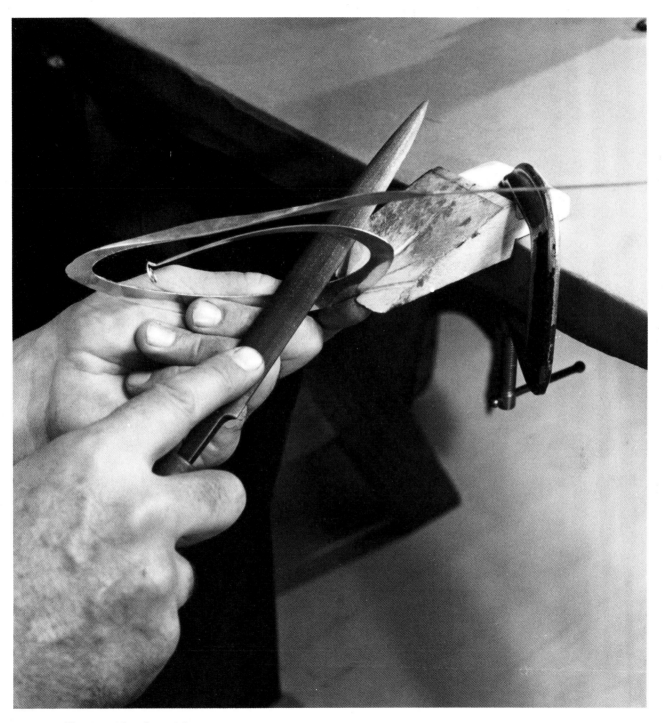

Figure 11. The edges of the forged planes are filed smooth.

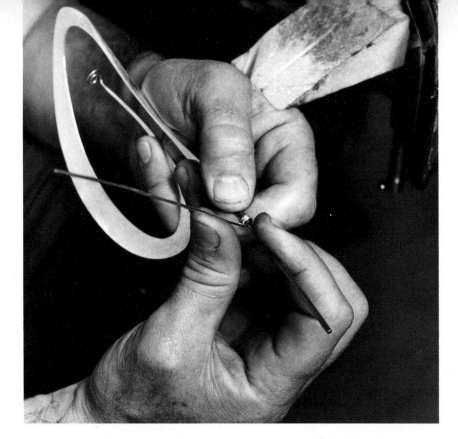

Figure 12. The coil spring for the pin stem is bent around a steel mandrel.

cross peen reshaped and finished to a mirror surface. The three pliers I use are a forming, a hollow chop, and a ring-bending. My files are a No. 2 and a No. 6 1-inch hand file and a No. 2 and a No. 6 8-inch crossing. The buffs are a 5-inch loose muslin for tripoli and a 5-inch, lead center, loose fine muslin for rouge.

To proceed with the piece, the shoulders left by rolling are hammered out on the anvil with the planishing end, and the piece is straightened. (Figure 3) The catch end and the pin stem are rounded up, first by striking with the planishing end of the hammer on the corners of the silver to make an eight-sided section; then, while rotating the piece slowly, by striking it lightly to eliminate all corners and make it round. (Figure 4) The ends are buffed with tripoli, but no point is made on the stem yet, for it is to be cut back to proper length later.

The forging begins at the widest point, and a curve at this point is first set by placing the silver wire over a depression in a wood stump and hammering it into the hole until a curve is formed. (Figure 5) With the peen striking parallel to the wire, I then forge the piece, first from the front, then the back, to spread the silver to maximum width (which can be as much as four times the original dimension). (Figure 6) Next I set

Figure 13. The nearly
completed piece is buffed
with tripoli.

the left-hand curve. Like the first curve this is started over a depression on the stump, which has several depressions of varying radii, but it is finished with the ring-bending pliers, as the curve has too sharp a turn to be done easily with the hammer alone. (Figure 7) After it is formed, I forge this curve and planish it. (Figure 8)

At this point, the spiral is made, in order to get that end out of the way so that the right side can be forged. Using the forming and hollow chop pliers, I make a 90-degree turn upward in the silver in the same plane as the piece and at the shoulder between the 17 gauge and the 11 gauge. (Figure 9a) I start forming the spiral at the end of the wire, curving downward. This is the tightest part of the curve. (Figure 9b) I continue forming the spiral to about one and a half turns in all, keeping an even distance between curves and keeping the spiral true and round. (Figure 9c) The spiral will act as a sort of safety catch to hold the pin stem point. Next, the one vertical plane is forged, by turning the wire 90 degrees (Figure 10), then the remaining horizontal planes. Final adjustment of the curves is done from the back by striking along the side opposite to the direction I want the metal to move.

The next step is to file the edges (*not* the full hammered planes!) with the No. 2 and then the No. 6 hand and crossing files. (Figure 11) Control of line is important, so I usually do the inside curve first and then shape the outside to the inside line. I draw-file the inside curves and, lastly, hit all edges with a No. 6 file to remove burrs. It should not be necessary to do much filing, for the real shaping is done with the hammer: with careful hammering, uneven or bumpy edges can be avoided.

Now I add a coil to the base of the pin stem, partially to serve as a spring for the pin and partially as a decorative touch that seems to balance the spiral catch. The pin stem coil is turned around a steel mandrel in order to make sure that the coils will be uniform. (Figure 12)

The pin stem itself has been left straight up to this point to reduce the chance of catching the piece on the polishing wheel during buffing. After buffing, which I do with tripoli from two or more directions (Figure 13), I use the forming pliers to make the final curve in the pin stem to set it in place; I cut the stem to the proper length, file a point, and make small adjustments. Then I polish with rouge, following the lines of the piece as much as possible and doing the edges first, the back plane next, and the front last. When polishing, I handle the piece with a clean cloth. Finally, I wash the pin in a solution of hot water, detergent, and ammonia; hot rinse it; and dry it in jeweler's sawdust. Ordinarily, a pin like this takes about two and a half hours to make.

Gold Neckpiece. 14-karat yellow gold, amethyst; forged and split single unit with constructed setting; 8" high x 8½" wide x 7" deep

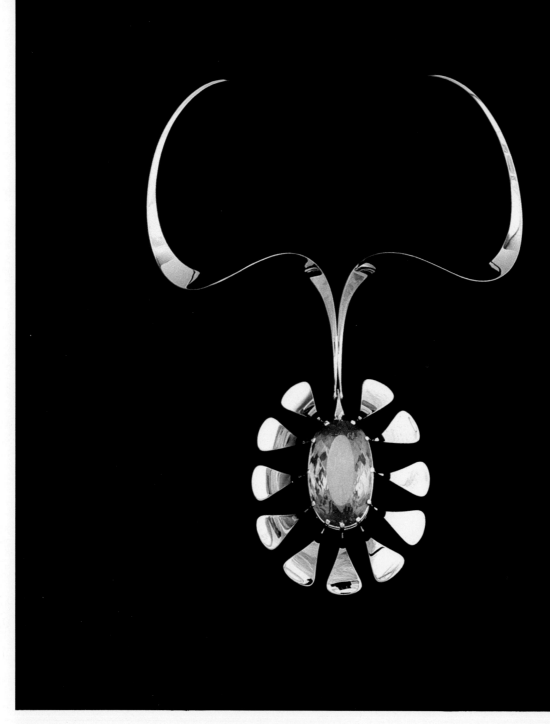

Gold Neckpiece. 14-karat yellow gold, 133-karat topaz; two-piece
forged construction, with eleven cast pieces in stone setting

Gold Neckpiece
14-karat yellow gold, forged and fused casting shot; front piece is two interlocking sections; 10½" long x 5" wide

Gold Ring
18-karat yellow gold, rhodolite garnet; cast

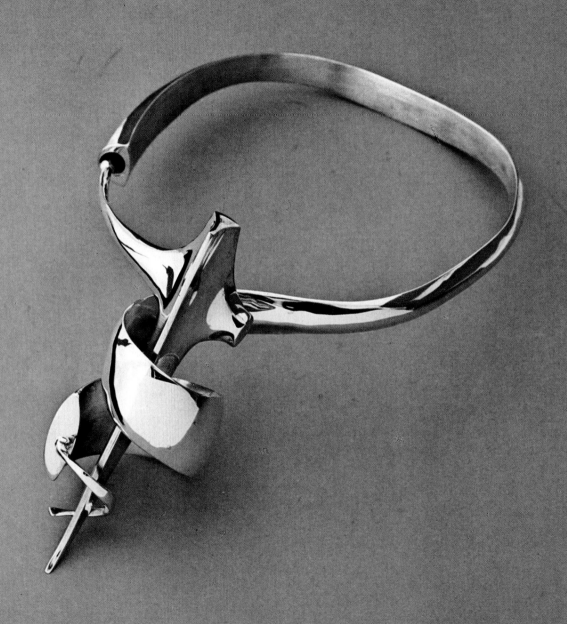

Helicoid Neckpiece
Heikki Seppä

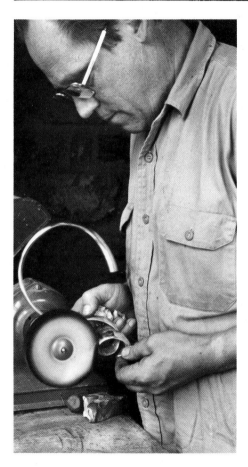

Heikki Seppä is an internationally known jeweler who began his career in Denmark. He has continually sought to develop a greater variety of forms in the work of metalsmiths. For his piece here he has used a shell construction that breaks away from the traditional bowl-box-cylinder syndrome that has often restricted jewelers.

Heikki Seppä was born in Finland. He studied at the Helsinki Goldsmith School and the Central School of Industrial Art in Helsinki and received the diploma for the Master status from the Finnish Governmental Agency. He further studied at Georg Jensen Silversmiths in Copenhagen, Denmark, and at the Cranbrook Academy of Art in Bloomfield Hills, Michigan.

His work has been exhibited in many shows, among which are Fiber–Metal–Clay U.S.A. in Wichita, Kansas, 1962; solo exhibitions at the Craft Alliance Gallery in Saint Louis, Missouri, 1966 and 1973; the Industrial Fair in Munich, Germany, 1968 and 1970; Goldsmith '70 in Saint Paul, Minnesota, 1970; the Art Gallery of Ontario in Toronto, 1971; the DeCordova Museum in Lincoln, Massachusetts, Goldsmith '74 at the Smithsonian Institution in Washington, D.C., Profile '74 at Humber College, in Toronto, Ontario, and the City Art Museum in Saint Louis, Missouri, 1974.

His work is in the collections of the Evansville Museum of Art and Science in Evansville, Indiana; the State University of Texas in El Paso; Texas Tech University Museum in Lubbock; the State University of Illinois in Normal; Washington University, Steinberg Galleries, in Saint Louis, Missouri; and numerous private collections.

He is a member of the Society of North American Goldsmiths.

Heikki Seppä has taught at the Louisville Art Center, Louisville, Kentucky; the School of Fine Arts, Washington University, Saint Louis; Penland School of Crafts; and numerous summer programs in the United States and Canada. He lives in Saint Louis, Missouri.

Helicoid Neckpiece. Sterling silver construction

I was born and raised in the region of Finland called Carelia. As a young boy I used to make all my own toys. I was very handy with an axe, a saw, and a knife. I liked whittling and carving forms in the soft wood of alder and mountain ash. Some well-meaning people noticed my skills and urged me to enroll in the Goldsmith School in the capital. I did, and moved to Helsinki.

The Goldsmith School was a wondrous place where I hoped to learn to make all sorts of personal items, not only for myself, but for others—for sale. I wanted to become an artist, a contributor to society and to mankind. By the time the four years of study were over, I was convinced that metalsmithing should be my life's activity. I enjoyed working and I was awarded some prizes for my designs and pieces.

After graduation, two of us students were selected to go to Denmark to work and study at the famous Georg Jensen's Silversmiths. We stayed a little over a year and learned how the professionals did it. We felt very important to be able to share in something that the whole world was paying attention to. Life was firming up for us.

However, I had just gotten married, and times were really rough. We couldn't find a place to live, so, in 1951, we moved to Canada, to British Columbia, where I put my childhood skills to use and built us a house.

We stayed in British Columbia for nine years. I taught metalsmithing in a local civic center. Then, since I wanted to learn more, I went to Cranbrook Academy of Art in Bloomfield Hills, Michigan, as a special student. That was the start of my academic teaching career, which took me to Louisville, Kentucky, for the next five years. There I learned to deal with buying customers. I worked hard, taught, and worked on my own. My work still consisted of one-of-a-kind pieces, but it was very easily salable, well-made jewelry and functional silver.

In 1965 Washington University offered a position in Saint Louis. I'm now an associate professor of fine arts there and a coordinator of metalsmithing studies.

With my major and graduate students I have collaborated on several issues in the field of metalsmithing. The strongest of these is the lack of attention paid to forms. Metalsmithing is traditionally divided into two major areas: one that concerns itself with surface enrichment and one that concerns itself with underlying form. Surface treatment has been developed to a very sophisticated and varied degree—but the forms have hardly changed since the days of Benvenuto Cellini. Like an old house that he paints every year, the metalsmith has been polishing and coruscating the same forms for a hundred years. With the knowl-

Figure 1. Idea sketches are drawn, with details and dimensions.

Figure 2. A strip of silver about 2.5 cm x 60 cm is cut with snips from sheet about 0.8 mm (20-gauge) thick.

edge and skills of today, the contemporary metalsmith has been long due for a change in his basic approach to the use and handling of precious metals.

The reason for the neglect of form can be traced to the fact that there has been no dialogue to teach anything other than raising bowls, setting stones, soldering cylinders, forging, box making, and so on. The vocabulary is undeveloped and has left out such exercises as go into making spouts, handles, finials, bases, nodes, and lids. The available books show and talk of only three starting approaches in sheet stock handling. These are cylinders, bowl raising, and box making. It is only by chance that the student finds out other ways to manipulate sheet stock.

For that reason, we feel that a new, liberating vocabulary is needed to assist in the form revolution. Generic terms to describe forms could not only promote a better understanding of the forms themselves, but would eliminate the reference to already known objects. As it is now, we talk about a "bowl shape," when we should say a "domical form." "Boat shape" should be a "cymbiform" or "scaphoid"; "wedge shape" should be a "sphenoid." Cuneiform, aliform, helicoid, hyperbolic parabola, and many more are all useful terms in design. Perhaps the strength of these terms lies in their mutability. In the designing stages a helix can be turned into a helicoid, meaning not quite, or like a helix; "helical" and "helicoidal" are other forms of the root word. The word "aliform," meaning "a form with wings," also has other forms, such as "alate" and "alated." The

Figure 3. After the first shell of the helicoid is hammered into shape, the pattern for the second one is taken from the edges of the first, on a strip of paper. The pattern is then trimmed to the pencil lines and used to cut a new strip of silver, from which the corresponding second shell is hammered.

Figure 4. Forming is done on metal stakes with wooden mallets or on wooden stakes with metal hammers.

meaning of the generic term is freer and less dictating than the reference to an actual object. It allows the designer to transform the concept of a wing, for example, into an abstract state, whereas the use of the word "wing" directly implies a bird or airplane and imprisons the designer.

I like to define jewelry in a way that is not common. I don't think of jewelry as decoration or body ornamentation, and least of all as miniature sculpture. I consider it personal art. I reason with the statement this way: Good jewelry is much less susceptible to the fluctuations of style and fashion than other art forms. It is a stable reflector of those intimate, personal, individual preferences that no other art form can reach. Jewelry, being personal art—in contrast to public art (sculpture, painting, architecture)—seldom needs to be justified by its owner. It is perhaps the most intimate repository of ideas, beliefs, concepts, and convictions of any art form. Jewelry makes its presence felt by visual, kinetic, tactile means in every wearer's life. Like the individuals who wear it, it should always be one-of-a-kind.

Generally I don't like to see, hear, or handle my work once I've

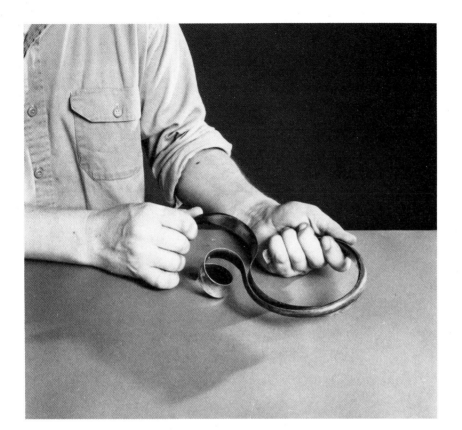

Figure 5. The two shells are fitted together for soldering. This must be done carefully and accurately to avoid distorting the form.

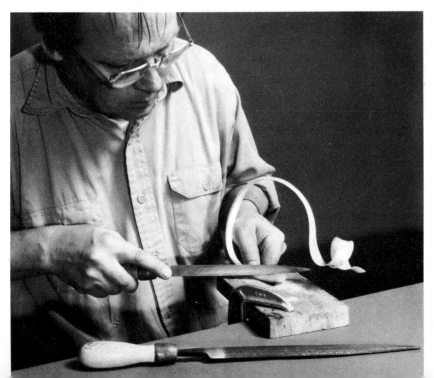

Figure 6. Solder faces are filed true for a sound seam and a snug fit.

finished it. The most distasteful task is to try to justify or tell about it. I can't afford to fall in love with my work. The pieces I make are like mileposts. If I stop at one, it might mean that I'll pitch a tent and the trip will be over. To keep going I must forget any mileposts that I have passed. Eventually I'll have to stop anyway; I'm sure I'll see one sooner or later that will make me stop.

The piece I have made here is a neckpiece, in a technique called shell structuring. It is made completely of easily formed shells, which are fitted together and soldered. The piece is hollow and light, yet strong. It would be more accurate to call it a "bi-shell," since it consists of two shells put together. The form itself is a reverse helicoid—the direction of the main curve is reversed to go in the opposite way, around the neck. The locking device is also a hollow shell, with the generic name "aliform." The aliform itself is made of three simple shells.

By sketching I record and preserve ideas that visit my mind. (Figure 1) I try to capture all the ideas, good or bad. Once I have a chance to look at them in my sketchbook I can either modify them with new ideas or discard them completely. Sketching is like a distillation process. I eliminate all the bad stuff and often purify an idea that never even gets sketched but prolongs its visit in my mind. In this case I reserve the right to subject my intended neckpiece to changes, possibly dictated along the way by the technique and material. I always sketch full-size.

From the sketched design I take measurements and develop a paper pattern for the piece. This pattern must allow enough material for the curves and bends, which in most cases are rather difficult to represent by a flat silhouette. This is one important point in interpreting the sketch. Each person does it differently.

Once the flat pattern is tested and tried, it is glued on the silver sheet. Snips or a jeweler's saw are used to free the silver strip from the sheeting. (Figure 2) Since the structure is going to be very strong, it needs only a relatively thin sheet for its construction. I have used 0.8-mm-thick silver. In addition to its pure, soft white color, silver is a very supple metal to work with. It can be easily formed, joined, and finished.

To form the helicoid I use an end grain of soft wood as a base, either a stump or a piece of four-by-four lumber. I prefer the non-resinous woods because they don't leave scum on the metal. I use a metal hammer when I work on the wooden surfaces, and a wooden mallet when I use metal stakes and forms. I mallet the silver over the form until it is shaped in a curve according to the design; then I take a stake

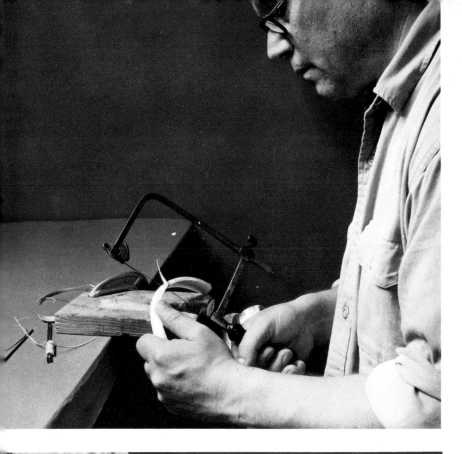

Figure 7. Once the two pieces are mated and soldered, the excess material is sawed or snipped off. Smoothing with a file follows. The end caps are soldered on in the same manner.

Figure 8. (*left*) Minor volume alterations on the sketch are made to fit the aliform inside the helix.

Figure 9. One of the three shells of the aliform is planished on a hornstake.

with a well-polished metal surface, curved or straight—depending on my form—and a hammer, and I planish the piece to remove all the lumps and irregularities caused by the forming process. This leaves the silver work-hardened and springy.

I can now put a piece of paper over the edges of the first shell of the helicoid and scribe the new pattern for the second shell. (Figure 3)

To make the second shell, I hammer the silver with a wooden mallet over a hyperbolic paraboloid metal stake. This shell is the same as the first, except that it is bent in the opposite direction. When the two shells are put together, they will form a structure resembling a clam shell—a bi-shell, in my terminology—a piece that is completely hollow. (Figure 4)

Fitting the two pieces together is much easier than it looks. (Figure 5) The first shell is usually the stronger of the two. It is also still in the work-hardened state. The second shell can be formed close to the first one, but the last fitting is done with binding wire. I tie the two pieces face to face with 0.8-mm soft iron wire, spacing it about every inch along the length of the helicoid. The fit may not be perfect yet, but when the second shell is annealed against the work-hardened first shell, the binding wires will pull it into a tighter fit. Annealing may be done

Figure 10. The two primary shells of the aliform are fitted and soldered together before the third shell is made.

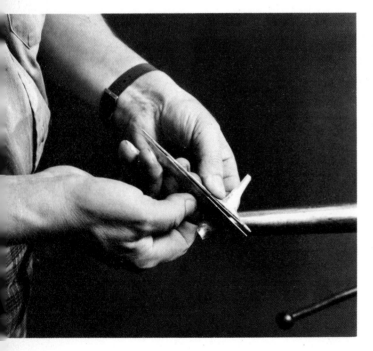

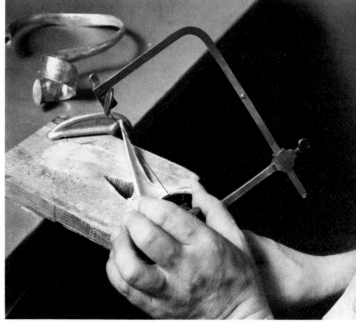

Figure 11. After the three shells of the aliform are soldered together, the excess material is trimmed off with a jeweler's saw, then filed smooth.

Figure 12. The helicoid and the aliform are now ready for removal of all file marks. This is done with fine abrasive papers or with a polishing lathe.

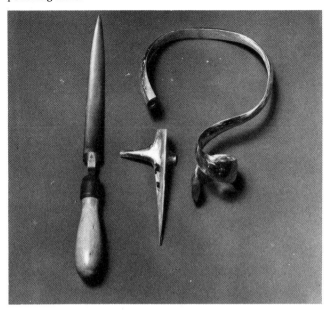

Figure 13. Pumice powder mixed with motor oil (to keep the powder from flying away as dust) is a good abrasive when used on a rotating felt lap. All the tool marks are removed until the surface of the neckpiece is free of any nicks or scratches.

with a gas-air or acetylene torch. It will release the work-hardening and render the metal soft again.

After annealing, the two shells are separated again for still closer fitting with a file. (Figure 6) They must be cleaned and retied with wire for soldering. To make the soldering easier, the second shell has been cut a little larger than the first. This leaves a narrow ledge on which to place the solder. It also makes tying easier, because small nicks can be filed in the ledge to keep the binding wires in place.

After tying, the piece is fluxed inside and out. (The flux maintains the cleanliness during heating.) Then the torch is played over a large area to heat the shells. If the piece is uniformly hot, the capillary attraction on the seam makes the solder flow easily. Later the ledge and the surplus solder are trimmed off with snips or a jeweler's saw. (Figure 7) Filing follows, to remove all the hammer marks and other tool marks. The helicoid is now a unit, strong and light.

Now I return to my sketch to make some minor alterations. (Figure 8) I have decided to let the excess metal be part of the piece rather than cutting it away, which means that the helix part is much wider than I have sketched it. To fit the aliform through the center of the helix

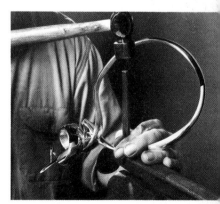

Figure 14. The maker's mark and the quality mark are stamped on.

and still have it function as a gate for the neck to enter, I have to modify its appearance a little. These are the liberties that you reserve for the time when you can evaluate the results and change them. I have also been concerned about the weight of the piece, but now it looks as if the piece will be strong, light, and wearable.

I proceed to lay out the paper pattern for one of the three shells of the aliform and cut it out from a silver sheet stock. Once this shell is formed it must be planished (Figure 9) to firm it up for the second pattern, which is cut out the same way and also formed and planished. At this point the two main shells of the aliform can be soldered together at the straight juncture, the seam. (Figure 10) Now the back of the aliform must be closed. The third shell is developed on a piece of paper by tracing the outline of the two joined shells, and transposed to yet another silver sheet stock. It is cut a little oversize to make soldering and fitting easier. It is also necessary to adjust the overall volume of the aliform so that it can be fitted inside the helix later with a small eyelet. This will be done even more accurately at the time the surplus ledge of the third shell is trimmed off. (Figure 11)

Now a small, solid silver bar with a ball end must be soldered to the right arm of the aliform; it will reach from the inside of the helix to the other end of the helicoid. This bar is forged and soldered on before buffing and polishing. A small socket in the end cap of the neck part of the helicoid will receive the ball end of the extension bar, which will provide a secure closing for the neckpiece. The aliform itself will be attached to the helix by means of two 1.5-mm eyelets, which will allow the aliform and extension bar to rotate and thus form the opening and closing mechanism.

At this point it is necessary to file and scrape the surfaces free of all other tool marks and excess solder. I prefer to use two different cuts of file. I start with a No. 2 cut file and remove all the rough material from the surfaces. Then I go over the piece again with a No. 4 cut, or if I can buy one, a No. 6 file. In places where the files don't fit, as in the concave sides of the aliform, I use a sharp steel tool called a scraper. (Figure 12)

To remove all the file marks I prepare a couple of gallons·of medium grade pumice powder. I mix the powder with a little No. 20 motor oil. This will bind the powder so that it doesn't fly in the air in the form of dust. The oil also makes the powder adhere to the piece and lets the felt wheels buff better. The felt wheels, or buffs, come in many sizes, hardnesses, and shapes; they are rotated in a tapered spindle that

Figure 15. The piece is now buffed to a high luster with fine aluminum oxide on a soft muslin buff. Sometimes rouge is used.

Figure 16. *(below left)* Small eyelets have been soldered on corresponding parts of the helicoid and the aliform, to attach the two pieces and provide an adjustable neck opening. Minor alignments are made to facilitate the opening and closing.

Figure 17. *(below)* The neckpiece is now closed. The aliform has a small knob at the end of one arm, which fits into a socket in the end cap of the helicoid.

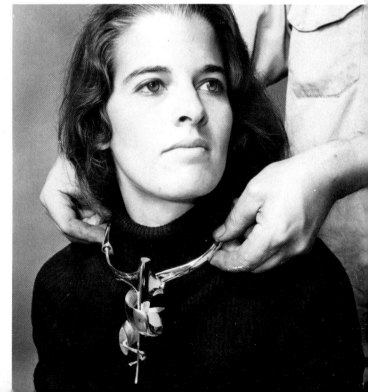

Figure 18. The final step is to join the eyelets together. Since the finished piece is hollow, it is very light and wearable.

is attached to a $^1/_2$ hp motor with a relatively slow speed, about 1700 rpm. The slow speed allows the pumice to cut into the metal without polishing it bright. This will speed the removal of the file marks and will leave the piece with a smooth but not shiny (nonglabrous) finish. (Figure 13)

After washing the piece with soap and water, I inspect it for any flaws in the seams and surfaces. I also decide on the type of final finish at this time. With shell structures, the surfaces can be treated in many different ways, but since my emphasis is on the form, and not the surface, I want to leave the form as unembellished as possible, in order to draw attention to it. I have decided to polish the whole piece to a very high shine, but I will leave the inside wall of the helicoid with a dull finish, which can be produced simply by rubbing the surface in one direction with dry pumice powder.

In order legally to be identified as sterling silver, the neckpiece has to be stamped. (Figure 14) Along with the sterling quality mark, I must also stamp my own mark, to guarantee that the piece is in fact sterling silver and nothing else. The stamp is also very important for the future identification. Art made from precious metals has a tendency to last a long time. The more direct information a piece carries, the easier it is to identify it historically. The stamping also deters fraudulent claims as to the material content of the piece.

I have now performed the last fitting for size on the aliform and have soldered the eyelets in place, one on the back of the aliform and one on the corresponding place on the helix. The final polishing takes place on a polishing motor, which is twice as fast as the pumice and oil motor—3400 rpm, or, to be more accurate, 5,000–7,000 feet per minute of buffing surface. It is the surface speed, not the rpm, that counts. I use a soft muslin cloth buff six inches in diameter, with a lead center. (Figure 15)

The surface speed of the buff is calculated thus:
$$C = D\pi.\ Ft./Min. = C\ R.P.M.\ \frac{in.\ p.\ m.}{12}$$

Circumference = 6" x 3.14 = inches of travel per one revolution (18.84 inches)
Inches of travel one minute = 18.84 x 3400 = 65,056 inches
Feet per minute = $\frac{65,056}{12}$ = 5421 feet per minute of surface speed

For effective buffing and polishing it is essential to know what different buffs do, and what factors influence the results. Highly polishing rag buffs and compounds are often used prematurely. High polish means that very little material is removed from the surface. Polishing itself is often a combination of slow removal of the surface and burnishing. The fibers of a loose buff have a beating and dragging action, which causes a slight flow of the surface molecules. The frictional heat, produced on the contact surface, aids the action and tends to cause a slight heat treatment effect on the piece.

For the final polishing compound I use 40-XXXX-grade aluminum oxide, which produces a good mirror finish. I could improve the finish a little by using red rouge—that is, iron oxide (rust)—but the process is so messy that I often skip it. For a really untouchable surface on silver I could use lamp-black and kerosene, but that would be even dirtier than rouge. Too high a polish is a short-lived pleasure on pieces that are to be handled by human beings.

I use a model for the final adjustment of the opening and closing mechanism. (Figure 16) The piece should be relatively easy to open and close; otherwise it gets to be a bother to wear and own.

The size of a neckpiece tends visually to exaggerate the size of the head. If the neckpiece is wider than the cheekbones or temple bones, it tends to make the head look smaller. Conversely, if the neckpiece is smaller than the cheek- or temple bones, the head looks bigger. For normal proportions the width of the neckpiece should be about the same width as the wearer's head.

I like to make my solid neckpieces so that they touch the wearer's shoulders at all points. (Figure 17) The piece should not span any part of the neckline, but should rest touching the roots of the neck firmly. Every wearer has a different neckline. Once a neckpiece is fitted, the wearer can hop up and down, lift her arms, and turn her head, and the neckpiece will always return to the same place. This might be the reason that solid-band neckpieces are not available on the commercial market; they must be fitted, and that's not usually possible in mass marketing. One-of-a-kind, individually made and fitted neckpieces are always striking additions to the attire.

Weight is much less of a factor in a neckpiece than, for instance, in a ring or an earring. Moreover, this piece is large in volume but weighs only five ounces.

When making the neckpiece it is easiest to polish and generally finish the work while the piece is still in separate parts. Thus, the last thing to do is to assemble the finished parts. Here there is only one operation: with a pair of pliers I join the aliform to the helicoid by closing the eyelets upon each other (Figure 18), and the piece is finished.

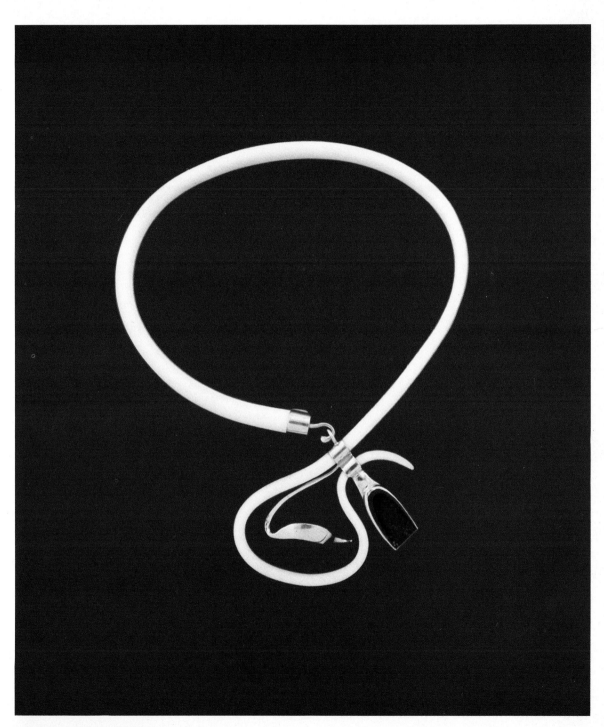

Teflon and Silver Neckpiece
Teflon, silver, jasper

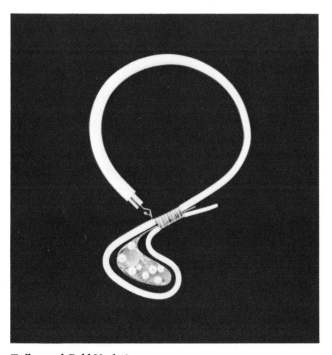

Teflon and Gold Neckpiece
Teflon, reticulated 14-karat
gold, pearls

Gold and Tourmaline Neckpiece
14-karat gold, micated
watermelon tourmaline

Gold Neckpiece. 14-karat gold, green
aventurine, nickel bronze, smoky quartz

Glossary of Jewelry-Making Terms

Annealing: A process of heat-treating a metal to a temperature below its critical stage. This is done mainly to relieve residual stresses, but also to render the metal soft for further working in a cold state.

Bezel: A band of metal surrounding a stone or other material that acts as a holding device or an outline.

Buffing: A process of using abrasives and polishing materials attached to a disk made of cotton, muslin, and other materials sewn together in layers. Buffing involves very little removal of metal. Its purpose is to achieve a finely polished surface.

Burnisher: A polishing tool made of steel, hematite, agate, or bloodstone in a variety of shapes. The tool is rubbed vigorously over the surface of the metal, using a lubricant to prevent scratching. The tool itself is always of a rounded cross-section and is kept at a high degree of polish to produce best results.

Chasing: A process of defining or texturing the surface of the metal on the front side, using chasing tools.

Dapping: The process of hammering small semicircular metal forms to produce domed or hemispheric cross-sections.

Dapping Punch: A tool with a highly polished round knob on the end that is used to dome sheet metal. When the punch is used in a block of wood or lead, it produces rounded bumps on the surface of a sheet of metal; when used in a *dapping block*—a cube-shaped piece of steel with semicircular depressions of various sizes—the metal must first be cut into circular form before it can be domed with the punch.

Draw plate: A flat steel plate pierced with graduated openings for reducing the cross-section diameter of a piece of wire or for changing the shape of the cross-section. Annealed wire is pulled through successively smaller openings with the aid of a pair of draw tongs.

Electroforming: A process of building up metal on the negative pole in a plating solution by using a relatively high amperage.

Electroplating: A process of light build-up of metal thrown off a pure metal anode to an object on the negative pole by using a relatively low amperage.

Embossing: A process of shaping sheet metal by pressing it from the back into a wood or lead block, which has previously been carved or indented with the desired relief form. Embossing very thin sheet metal may be done directly on a soft pad of felt, leather, or newspaper without any prior form being determined.

Fabricating: A process of creating a piece by construction instead of casting.

Filing: A process of removing small amounts of unwanted metal; shaping and finishing metals. A forward-moving stroke is used while the metal is securely held.

Flux: A paste made primarily from borax, used in silversmithing for two purposes: to coat silver before it is heated in order to prevent the formation of heat scale on the surface; and to serve as an indicator of the temperature of the silver, since flux flows when heated to 1100 degress.

Heat scale: A dark gray, shadowy effect formed on the surface of sterling silver when the silver is subjected to intense heat, during either annealing or soldering. Sterling silver is an alloy containing copper; heat scale is formed by the oxidation of the copper under intense heat.

Jump rings: Small circles of wire used as connectors or links in chains of various kinds. They may be purchased commercially by the gross or made in small quantities by hand, using a steel mandrel the size of the inner diameter of the circle desired.

Oxidizing: A process of coloring or darkening the metal surface by use of chemicals.

Photofabrication: A process of applying photographic images to metal or other surfaces by use of photosensitive resist and etching or electroplating.

Pickle: A hot solution of sulfuric acid or a commercially available solution, used to remove dirt and flux from a just-soldered piece.

Planishing: A hammering process used for refining and finishing the surface of a piece of metal, to achieve smoothness and uniformity. The conventional planishing hammer has both a flat and a slightly domed face and is highly polished; the blows of the hammer are placed evenly and systematically over the entire surface.

Repoussé: A process of creating a surface design, in low or high relief, by beating out the shape of the metal, usually from the back, with punches and hammers.

Sawing: Cutting metal with the use of a saw frame and blade. During the sawing, the metal is held firmly on a V-board while the blade is guided along the outside edge of the design, leaving excess metal, which is later trimmed with a file.

Soldering: A process of joining pieces of metal with alloys that flow at a temperature lower than that of the metals being joined. Easy, medium, and hard solder flow at different temperatures.

Stitch: A small burr pulled up from the metal surface with a burin or graver. The burr acts as a positioner for holding another piece of metal in place, usually done in preparation for soldering.